Yesterday's People

Yesterday's People

LIFE IN CONTEMPORARY APPALACHIA

By Jack E. Weller

With a New Preface by the Author

THE UNIVERSITY PRESS OF KENTUCKY

Scholarly publisher for the Commonwealth,
serving Bellarmine College, Berea College, Centre
College of Kentucky, Eastern Kentucky University,
The Filson Club, Georgetown College, Kentucky
Historical Society, Kentucky State University,
Morehead State University, Murray State University,
Northern Kentucky University, Transylvania University,
University of Kentucky, University of Louisville,
and Western Kentucky University.

Editorial and Sales Offices: The University Press of Kentucky
663 South Limestone Street, Lexington, Kentucky 40508-4008

The Library of Congress has cataloged the first printing of this title as follows:

Weller, Jack E.
    Yesterday's People; life in contemporary Appalachia, by Jack E. Weller.
[Lexington] University of Kentucky Press [1965]
    xx, 163 p.   23 cm.
    Bibliographical footnotes.
    1. Mountain whites (Southern States)   2. Appalachian Region—Social
conditions   I. Title.
F210.W43   917.509143   65-27012

Library of Congress   [8506r85]rev

(ISBN 0-8131-0109-3)

Contents

PREFACE, THIRTY YEARS AFTER, *by Jack E. Weller*   vii

AN INTRODUCTORY NOTE, *by Rupert B. Vance*   ix

FOREWORD, *by Harry M. Caudill*   xiv

ACKNOWLEDGMENTS   xix

1   INTRODUCTION   1

2   THE HOMELAND OF THE MOUNTAINEER   9
     The Inroads of Poverty, 17
     The Rediscovery, 23

3   INTRODUCING THE MOUNTAINEER   28
     Individualism, 29
     Traditionalism, 33
     Fatalism, 37
     Seekers of Action, 40
     The Psychology of Fear, 44
     Person Orientation, 49

4   THE MOUNTAINEER IN HIS SOCIETY   58
     The Family, 59
     Children and the Family, 61
     The Training of Children, 64
     Mountain Youth, 68
     Marriage, 72

The Changing Role of the Sexes, 76
Adult Reference Group Life, 78
Leaving the Family, 82
The Reference Group and the Self, 83

5 THE MOUNTAINEER AND THE COMMUNITY   87
The Rural Mountaineer, 88
The Rural Community, 89
The Commercial Center and County Seats, 91
The Coal Camp, 92
Traits at Work in the Community, 94

6 THE MOUNTAINEER AND THE OUTSIDE WORLD 102
The World of Work, 102
Education, 107
Politics, 113
Medical Care, 116

7 THE MOUNTAINEER AND THE CHURCH   121
Historic Tendencies, 121
Religious Individualism and Self-Reliance, 124
Religious Traditionalism and Fatalism, 128

8 THE MOUNTAINEER AND THE FUTURE   134
The Forces of Change, 134
Obstacles to Change, 138
Some Beginning Points, 141
Evaluations and Conclusions, 150

APPENDIX   161

Preface, Thirty Years After

Thirty years ago *Yesterday's People* spoke to the life of the people in the Appalachian hills and valleys as well as to those interested in them. To my surprise, it became a best seller. Recently, at the request of the University Press of Kentucky, an update was suggested, noting changes in these later days. They have indeed been many.

Improved roads have made it easier for people to travel in and out of the area. In this way they have been able to take jobs in cities as well as continue their family relationships in the mountains. Those who remain within the mountains are also being changed by easier travel.

Coal mining, which formerly so devastated the land, is now making flat land available for housing and industry because of reclamation requirements. Coal trucks are required to be covered to prevent spillage along the highways. It is very gratifying to see such positive results from the legislative efforts to bring stripmining under control. Now, the new methods of mining coal preserve the land. Streams are clearer, and vegetation is growing on former stripped areas. Many dilapidated coal camps have been torn down, making way for new housing. More people own their own homes, and there is evidence of new pride in the appearance of mountain communities.

At the same time there are fewer jobs in the mines as giant machines have taken over. Many have had to move away to find work, greatly reducing the population. School children are now transported long distances to consolidated schools instead of using small, inadequate local schools.

In a real sense, then, the Appalachian people are largely integrated into the American scene. As they have moved into the mainstream of society, they have brought with them many lovely attributes—their closeness and caring for family, the genuineness of their concern for their neighbors, and their willingness to share with others even though they may be poor themselves.

In a way it is sad to see the passing of a subculture that was unique. Yesterday's People. They have enriched us by their lives and their love. They are indeed now a part of the "melting pot" of our nation, and they have brought to us a significant part of themselves to add to the "global village" that is the United States.

Jack E. Weller
May 1995

An Introductory Note

It is a cliché, no doubt, but many a publisher hopes every time he opens his mail to pick up an unsolicited manuscript that actually rings a bell. It happens so seldom that some forget it can happen. When the Reverend Jack Weller, a mountain minister, sent his manuscript in to the University of Kentucky Press, it happened. This was my conviction, too, when I was given a chance to read this book in advance of publication. I am very glad to be offered the opportunity to introduce the work.

Some books are made of other men's books; other books come directly out of experience. These are often the best books, for they are made from men's lives. This book comes out of a minister's thirteen years as missionary to churches in the Southern Appalachians. Because he came as a missionary, Mr. Weller brought the objectivity of the stranger. Finally, he came to know these people better than they knew themselves. Intimate involvement in the social life of a people does not necessarily reveal the meaning of that life to a native who has no standard of comparison, but for Mr. Weller there was always a background of the other life, the outside world with which he could make comparison. There are no schedules here; nothing is coded; few respondents are listed; only hundreds of unmentioned interviews that this minister carried on with parishioners, neighbors, acquaintances over a span of many years. The beauty of this book is that the whole thing remains completely informal but rings completely true.

Each year the Council of the Southern Mountains is attended by "delegates" from Chicago, Cincinnati, Detroit, and points north. Why is this? Social work executives and heads of city welfare programs come south to this meeting in order to learn about the problems migrants from the southern mountains offer to our great cities. First, our cities had to learn how to live with foreign immigrants; then they were faced with the migration of Negroes from the agricultural South; finally, they must adjust their programs to newcomers from the Southern Appalachians. It is my feeling that in Mr. Weller's little book they have been presented a key to the motivation, the folkways, the mores and the personality of these people.

The problems of the southern mountains have long been in and out of the public eye and now they are back again to stay. Practically all of the national denominations have supported missionary activities in the area and before the age of public schools many staffed and supported mountain academies. Health services were first taken to the mountains by the Frontier Nursing Service. These nurses rode horseback to deliver the babies of mountain mothers and were the first to bring maternal and child health services to these remote areas. Berea College remains a fine example of an institution especially adapted to mountain culture and needs.

Now the public agencies are stepping in and there is money in the budget for the Southern Appalachians. In 1961 President Kennedy signed the Area Redevelopment Act, a measure to help stranded rural and urban communities overcome chronic unemployment. The Cumberland plateau, practically all of West Virginia's counties, and other regions of the Appalachians were designated as redevelopment areas under the new act. New programs are now in operation. In West Virginia, a group of remote counties, organized under the Combined Extension Services of the University of West Virginia, have embarked on a program of development proposed and guided by core committees from the most mountainous counties. Under a grant from the Kellogg Foundation, the University of Kentucky is carrying integrated extension services to the thirty counties of the Cumberlands in an attempt to hasten redevelopment. The plan is to stimulate communities by these services, to inventory their needs and work toward alleviation.

The governor of North Carolina and his advisers secured the support of the Ford Foundation and other groups and established the North Carolina Fund with the aim of ending the cycle of poverty in North Carolina. All this has come to a climax in the Economic Opportunity Act in which President Johnson is attempting to mobilize a national attack on poverty. With administrative machinery at hand, with seed capital in sight, with a favorable climate of public opinion we come to a most important question. What is the way out? What road blocks remain?

Analyses of the Appalachians are no longer presented as portraits of quaint customs and surviving folklore. Nor is it sufficient to delimit subregions and analyze the effects of agriculture, mining and reforestation. The survey of the Appalachian region which our author frequently quotes devoted special attention to the attitudes of community leaders. The persons named as leaders turned out to be considerably ahead of the total population in education, property ownership, income, and age. Definitely these leaders were ahead of the people in pushing for change and development; they were activists and progressives; they are receptive to national values and contacts. If feasible plans and programs can be developed, it seems evident that they will have the support of community leaders.

What about the rank and file? It is here that Mr. Weller's book assumes its importance. He has attempted to give us an accounting of the personality and attitudes of the Appalachians' common man. If in some respects, it is not too encouraging, on the other hand, it is not completely discouraging. The upshot of the matter is that the mountain man has about the same attitudes and personality we would have if we were in his situation.

A change is overdue in our approach to the problems. The older studies of the region were more concerned with causation than with social change; they emphasized the static influence of tradition. They looked back to physical limitations, to isolation and inadequate resources and the crude modes of making a living. Thence the analysis moved forward to consider institutional adjustments and the attitudes of the people. Thus mountain isolation, which began as physical isolation enforced by rugged topography, became mental and cultural isolation, holding people in disadvantaged areas, resisting those changes that would bring them into contact with the outside world. The effect of conditions thus becomes a new cause of conditions, but the cause is now an attitude, not a mountain. If we devote attention to religion in the mountains we find that the differences found in mountain religion are in part the effect of conditions under which the people have lived. Not only is it an effect of these conditions, but the particular attitudes of religion may then operate to perpetuate these conditions. Thus if hard lives give rise to fatalism and fundamentalism these attitudes may operate to perpetuate fatalism. The transition from accepting things as they are to trying to make things better, involves the acceptance of a social gospel which has not yet reached the minds of all these people.

Since mountains are not likely to be moved, the new regionalism proceeds on the assumption that men can be moved. It is here that Mr. Weller's understanding proves most valuable indeed. If Mr. Weller leads us to believe that religion has not been a comfort and a support for the people of the mountains, he thereby gives us hope for change. Indeed one wonders in reading his pages if their religion actually brings them any happiness. Ofttimes their religion seems to be one of fear and anticipation of future punishment. Throughout this book, serving to bring human personality into the forefront, the crux of the problem is clear. To change the mountains is to change the mountain personality. Here Mr. Weller is not a pessimist; he is a realist who does not underestimate the task. We can do with more realism in the world today. I hereby suggest we move over and make a place for him.

Rupert B. Vance
*University of North Carolina
   at Chapel Hill
August 6, 1965*

Foreword

THE Appalachian mountaineers have been discovered and forgotten many times. They first attracted national attention during the Civil War. Their primitive agriculture disrupted by foragers and incessant guerrilla warfare, thousands of them straggled out of the mountains in search of food and shelter. General O. O. Howard, the director of the Bureau of Refugees, Freedmen and Abandoned Lands, called their plight to the attention of the White House, and President Lincoln told the General that after the war a way would be found to aid the poor mountain people whom the world had bypassed and forgotten for so long.

In the century since Lincoln's death much has happened to the mountaineers, but little has been done for them. Toward the end of the nineteenth century romanticists such as James Lane Allen and John Fox, Jr., sought out the highlanders and for a good many years the mountaineers, their "quaintness," their loves and their feuds were grist for occasional stories and magazine articles. More often than not the mountaineer emerges from the yellowed pages of that era as a sort of gallant knight, backward, illiterate, primitively housed and clad, but a nobleman all the same.

In the same years when the romanticists were at work pioneers in the infant science of sociology began to find their way along the mountain trails. Startled by a society frozen in many of the habits and mores of the frontier a century before, some of them described the mountaineers as "our contemporary ancestors," an appellation which implied that the mountaineer of 1890 was a carbon copy of his great grandfather of 1790.

Except for West Virginia, mountain counties are relatively uninfluential parts of the states in which they lie. This historic fact has caused the state-houses largely to ignore the highlanders except for occasional electioneering forays. On these jaunts the politicians titillated their backwoods listeners by telling them they were the "finest Anglo-Saxon stock in the world." This irrelevant nonsense garnered many votes but did nothing to alleviate any Appalachian problem.

But businessmen, too, discovered the mountaineers and their homeland. To the speculators of eighty years ago the mountaineers were geese to be plucked and, taking advantage of their ignorance and their long isolation from the rest of the world, the entrepreneurs acquired title to the vast wealth of Appalachia. For trifling sums immense stores of coal, petroleum, natural gas, limestone, and huge areas of land passed into the hands of capitalists in Philadelphia, Boston, New York, Cincinnati, and a dozen other cities. Thereafter the mountaineers lived in a region whose economic destiny was controlled by men who lived far away and who seldom saw the territory.

To the industrialists who opened the coal mines, set up the great saw mills, operated the quarries, built the railroads and hauled away the resources the population was a made-to-order source of cheap labor. Though fabulous wealth has been generated in Appalachia, the mountaineers' share in it has been held to a minimum.

This beautiful region of steep wooded hills, narrow valleys, and winding streams is a land of contradiction and tragedy. Appalachia has become synonymous with destitution and illiteracy. For example, in eastern Kentucky alone are six of the ten poorest counties in America. Yet, of all America's corporations none are more profitable than east Kentucky land companies. In 1964 one of them managed to retain as net profit 61 percent of its gross income. Another paid out as dividends 45 percent of its total receipts.

A combination of historic circumstances set the mountain people on the road to poverty amid riches. The first settlers brought a powerful strain of social anarchy derived in part from the philosophy of the Levelers, a revolutionary group which gave powerful support to Cromwell's Commonwealth. They moved inland from the coastal areas to escape restraint. They were stubborn, opinionated, and sometimes cruel. People had to have these qualities in order to survive on the tooth-and-talon frontier. The Appalachians became a great sponge which absorbed the backwoods people in large numbers. The mountain walls sheltered their strengths, their quirks, and their shortcomings from the rest of the world. They turned aside subsequent streams of human migration. In a century of isolation the Appalachian subculture was born.

Novelists, poets, sociologists, government bureaucrats, politicians, and industrialists have commented on the Appalachian mind. The harshest judgment of all was rendered by the English historian, Arnold Toynbee, who purported to find in the mountains a people who had reverted from civilization to barbarism. He dismissed them with this comment: "The modern Appalachian has . . . failed to hold his ground and has gone downhill in a most disconcerting fashion. In fact, the Appalachian 'mountain people' today are no better than barbarians. They have relapsed into illiteracy and witchcraft. They suffer from poverty, squalor and ill-health. They are the American counterparts of the latter-day White barbarians of the Old World—Rifis, Albanians, Kurds, Pathans and Hairy Ainus; but, whereas these latter are belated survivals of an ancient barbarism, the Appalachians present the melancholy spectacle of a people who have acquired civilization and then lost it."

Many people have told the Appalachian story—the feuds, the inadequate agriculture, the harsh life of the mining towns, the terrible mining accidents, the shocking illiteracy rate, the primitive school systems, the chronically high incidence of disease. Others have collected the songs and the tales which give life to the narrative. Jack Weller has performed a unique work of a different character. He has analyzed the Appalachian mind in a remarkably skillful manner. His book deals primarily with the people as they are, rather than with the complex forces which shaped them. He deals with the end result of initial backwoods intransigence followed by generations of isolation, poor schools, and governmental neglect. His analysis of the Appalachian mind and personality is likely to take its place as an analytical work comparable to *The Mind of the South* by W. J. Cash.

The nation will not be allowed again to forget its southern mountaineers. The long years of isolation are ending and millions of Americans will pass through the highlands. Impoverished by absentee ownership of the wealth and by an archaic agriculture, hordes of mountaineers are moving into the cities, carrying with them many attributes which arouse interest and resentment in urban areas. Population pressures will push a new torrent of people into Appalachia. Churchmen, bureaucrats, educators, students, vacationers will come in ever-growing numbers. For all of them *Yesterday's People* will prove to be an invaluable aid. It can open the door to a new understanding of our reticent mountaineers and their shy, often lonely children.

The book comes at a most opportune time. No serious effort to elevate American society can succeed without a far-reaching rejuvenation of Appalachia. And to accomplish this the nation must first find a fundamental understanding of the Appalachian psychology—of the mountaineer's quite different point of view. From Jack Weller—minister, student and keen observer—comes an important beginning toward that understanding.

Harry M. Caudill
Whitesburg, Kentucky
June 1965

Acknowledgments

To name one person as the author of a book is, I know now, something less than accurate. At least in the case of this one, many persons have contributed significantly to its appearing. Thus in this brief section I should like to name but a few of those persons who assisted so cheerfully and sacrificially in the task of bringing this book to reality.

My deep thanks go to the Reverend George Hall of the Colgate Rochester Divinity School teaching staff for the resources he found for me and for his encouragement to get started and keep going; to the United Presbyterian Church Board of National Missions for enabling me to take a semester for refreshment and study, and then for allowing me the time to finish the manuscript; to the Reverend Shubert Frye and Miss Betty Jean Patton of the Board for their assistance in so many ways; to the staff of the West Virginia Mountain Project for their encouragement and help in reading and criticizing as well as their willingness to take up extra duties in order to free me for writing; to Mr. Tom Parrish of the Council of the Southern Mountains for his fine work in editing; and to the people of Big Coal River Valley in West Virginia for these years of sharing their life with me in such wonderful ways. But perhaps most of all, I must acknowledge an overwhelming debt of gratitude to my wife, Jeanette, who read and re-read the manuscript, correcting mistakes and typing out my nearly illegible longhand a number of times.

There are many others who must go unnamed, but in whose debt I remain for their kind counsel.

Whitesville, West Virginia   Jack E. Weller

1.
Introduction

IT was thirteen years ago that I first came to Southern Appalachia, to a coal-mining area in the mountains of West Virginia. Work as a minister in a parish of the United Presbyterian Church called me there. As time went on and the period required for being accepted in a new community passed, and I still felt very much an outsider, I tried to analyze why I did not fit in as completely as I thought I should. Plans and methods that had been successful in other places were not effective here. Standard ways of working with individual persons, with committees, and with the community—ways that I had found satisfactory elsewhere— here failed completely. The people that I worked with seemed very eager for help and guidance, but their responses to my suggestions were sullen and sometimes almost resentful. I felt powerless to provide the answers or the leadership that the community needed. The people and I seemed to be living on two different levels of thinking, and at only a few places did we meet and understand one another. We spoke the same language, but we didn't communicate.

This realization came slowly to me—the realization that perhaps I was faced with a different way of life, a separate subculture based upon premises I was not aware of. Like most middle class Americans, I had always assumed that in our modern, mobile society we have a fairly homogeneous culture and that, generally, what makes us different is our income. Of course, we are all familiar with the usual

labels that the sociologists (professional and amateur) put
on us: lower class, middle class, professional class, upper
class. We even readily accept refinements of these divisions,
but these are presumed to mark us off according to "style"
of life, depending on how much income we have, how
much education we desire, what section of town we live
in, what kind of music and art and entertainment we allow
ourselves to enjoy, and how we spend our vacations and
leisure. We commonly assume that all of us in America,
wherever we live, have the same goals, the same ideals, the
same drives, and that most of these are oriented upward
("upward" usually means toward a higher income and toward the style of life that higher income allows).

But here I and the staff with whom I worked found these
assumptions did not hold. We were strangers in our own
country, among a people who did not seem to understand
us and whom we did not seem to understand. Gradually
we began to feel that our frustrations derived from our attempts to impose our own cultural assumptions on a people who did not share them. But how to understand this
mountain culture? Although a plethora of books had been
written on the mountaineer—romanticizing him, criticizing
him, deriding him—none had really tried to do more than
describe him, and this we could already do.

So we stand before the mountaineer, utterly baffled by
his peculiarities. Why isn't he like us? Why doesn't he
respond as we do, think as we do, live as we do? What are
his goals and hopes? Why, when he moves to the city and
is exposed to all the opportunities of city life, does he still
cling to his mountain ways? There are many unkempt
houses everywhere in Appalachia. Why doesn't the mountain man care how his house looks to others? There are a
multitude of children everywhere, unsupervised by any
adults. Doesn't the mountaineer care for his children? On

warm days there are people on every porch, sitting back as if they had not a care in the world when everybody says they are so poor. Are these people really so lazy? Have they no "get up and go"? And the central question of all is: Why are these folk living as they do, so contented that they do not seem even to want the help offered to them?

All these questions surely had answers, and I wanted to find them. I did not want simply to describe the mountaineer. I wanted to understand him, from his own level, not from mine. I did not want to impose my own middle class assumptions and judgments on his culture. In a conversation with the secretary of a doctor in a nearby city who has many patients from the surrounding mountain area, I explained that I wanted to understand what mountaineers think and hope for. "You mean they do?" she asked in all seriousness. This is the approach to mountaineers that the rest of America often seems to make. Mountain people do both think and hope for many things—but in a different way from middle class people. I wanted to find out why and how, and then put it down for the help of others who would work in the mountains. Most of the talking about the mountaineer is done by persons of another culture looking down on him. I wanted to understand him sympathetically, so that on hearing what I had to say he would reply, "Yes, that's the way we are."

The search for the answers began in the library. I soon discovered, however, that few studies of the kind I sought had ever been made. One book which catches the feelings and frustrations of mountain people, and which anyone studying the Appalachian South must read, is Harry Caudill's *Night Comes to the Cumberlands*. It is a lucid and fascinating study by an insider of the culture.

Another book gave me many of the tools and concepts I needed. *The Urban Villagers*, by Herbert J. Gans, is a study of the West End of Boston, its people and problems, before urban renewal moved in to "restore" the area. On reading Gans's descriptions of the patterns of life, the organization, and motivations of these second- and third-generation people from southern Italy, I felt my excitement rise. Here, at last, was a study that was trying to understand a people face to face, not to describe or evaluate them from the vantage point of another culture. "Actually, most of the talking has usually been done by the upper level; the people of the lower one sit by quietly, and even sullenly, often without listening. Thus, although I came to the West End from the upper level, I have tried to describe the way of life of lower-level people as they might describe it themselves if they were sociologists. In a sense, then, I am reporting to the upper level for them and urging that they be given more consideration when policy decisions are made."[1]

As I read *The Urban Villagers*, illustrations from my own work flooded to my mind. Vaguely understood incidents that had happened in the mountains began to make sense. In fact, I would urge readers of this book to follow up with Gans's study for a fuller treatment and deeper insights into the culture of the West Enders, who are so much like the people of Southern Appalachia. Gans describes the Boston West Enders as belonging to neither the lower nor the lower middle class. The lower class he describes as pathological, since it does not face and solve the problems of life in an adequate manner[2]—a description that does not fit the people of the West End, nor does it fit the great majority of Southern mountaineers. The West Enders are not lower middle class, for they have a homogeneous style

[1] Herbert J. Gans, *The Urban Villagers* (New York: Free Press of Glencoe, 1962), p. x.
[2] Gans, p. 269.

of life and behavior patterns that are utterly different. Gans suggests that there is a "working-class" subculture which fits in between the lower class and the lower middle class.[3] His description of this working class characterizes amazingly well the Southern mountaineer. It also seems to fit, in more or less degree, certain rural and inner-city people. As I shared my findings with inner-city pastors, they sensed a strong kinship between the working class culture Gans describes and their own people. This society —it is a kind of folk class—seems to appear whenever people exist in an environment which has limited or defeated them, whether it be in Appalachia, rural America, the inner city, or southern Italy.

Later I shall contrast various characteristics of the folk culture with those of the middle class. A chart in the appendix notes in detail some of these typical differences. Dr. Marion Pearsall of the University of Kentucky has also developed a most interesting chart, giving these differences from another point of view, and she has graciously consented to allow it to be reprinted here, where it can provide a glimpse into subsequent discussion.

Let it be said forcefully at this point, however, that there are widespread differences in culture in southern Appalachia. More than a generation ago, John C. Campbell noted that there are "difficulties in the way of writing of a people who, while forming a definite geographical and social group, were by no means socially homogeneous."[4] There is a middle class as well as a professional class in the mountains, and both have much the same characteristics as these classes anywhere else. They contrast with the folk class, which exists side by side with them. No one

[3] Gans, p. 25.
[4] *The Southern Highlander and His Homeland* (New York: Russell Sage Foundation, 1921), p. xiv.

SOME CONTRASTING VALUE ORIENTATIONS

Underlying Question	Southern Appalachian	Upper-middle Class (Professional)
What is the relation of man to nature (and supernature)?	Man subjugated to nature and God; little human control over destiny; fatalism	Man can control nature or God works through man; basically optimistic
What is the relation of man to time?	Present orientation; present and future telescoped; slow and "natural" rhythms	Future orientation and planning; fast; regulated by the clock, calendar, and technology
What is the relation of man to space?	Orientation to concrete places and particular things	Orientation to everywhere and everything
What is the nature of human nature?	Basically evil and unalterable, at least for others and in the absence of divine intervention	Basically good, or mixed good and evil; alterable
What is the nature of human activity?	Being	Doing
What is the nature of human relations?	Personal; kinship-based; strangers are suspect	Relatively impersonal; recognize non-kin criteria; handle strangers on basis of roles

should assume that all people living within Appalachia bear the stamp of this folk culture, or that I am describing all the people in the region. One might even go so far as to say that any Appalachian person who is willing to read such a study as this hardly qualifies to be included in it.

Even so, it is true that most people living within Appalachia (except for those who have lived in its cities for generations) have come out of this folk culture and so share it as a background, if nothing else. When I described the folk culture to a businessman in an Appalachian city, a man indigenous to the area, he noted that many of the middle class persons who work for him still exhibit strong marks of it.

What is described in this book certainly will not fit accurately every situation, every area, or every person in the mountains. Many of the traits described are common to other groups in American society as well. I am portraying some general tendencies of behavior in the mountaineer, indicating what I feel to be some basic differences between his subculture and that of middle class America and suggesting some implications for persons and groups—government, educational, church, welfare, industrial, and others—trying to work in these hills.

The greatest challenge of Appalachia, and the most difficult, is its people. To quote Howard Odum: "To attempt to reconstruct [the South's] agriculture and economy without coming to grips with its folk culture and attitudes would be quite . . . futile."[5] It is the human resource that holds the promise of this great area, and it is the human resource that is most difficult to deal with, simply because so many factors and forces that we do not understand bear upon the human spirit. It is to this human factor that this

[5] *Southern Regions of the United States* (Chapel Hill: The University of North Carolina Press, 1936), p. 499.

book is aimed, with the hope that those who have rediscovered Appalachia may not run roughshod over a people
who have already suffered too much of such treatment at
the hands of outsiders; that the tremendous values of this
mountain culture may not too quickly be cast aside; that
those who labor may not be discouraged if what they have
proposed and worked for fails because it runs counter to
the culture.

This book has emerged not from a specific study by one
trained in the field of sociology, but from thirteen years'
experience as a pastor among mountain people—experience
which has given me a deep feeling for them, and, I trust,
some insights into them. These years have been spent working with these folk of all ages, visiting in their homes, eating with them, sharing their deepest trials in time of tragedy and death, counseling the youth, and involving myself
as totally as I could in every area of their lives. Some mountain people, no doubt, will read hostility into these pages;
some may infer criticisms that were never implied; some
will mistakenly believe that I am characterizing all Appalachian dwellers. Some may feel that when I say they are
different I mean they are inferior; some may think that I
am trying to make them like everybody else when they
don't want to be. I hope this may not be the case, for I
have tried to share my understanding of the mountaineer's
life, his goals, and what makes his culture different from
general American culture in the hope that I could help
others work more effectively with him.

2.
The Homeland of the Mountaineer

Early in our nation's life the region we now call Appalachia became a problem: it was a block to settlers moving westward. The long ridges of the old mountains, which run for 1,300 miles from Vermont to northern Alabama, presented a formidable barrier to westward movement. These mountains are not high, as mountains go—Mt. Mitchell, the highest, rises not quite 6,700 feet—but they are steep and rugged and continue range after range.

The eastern edge of the Southern Appalachians is formed by the Blue Ridge Mountains, which rise steeply from the broad Piedmont that stretches toward the coast. In the Great Smokies and the Black Mountains, which together reach a width of a hundred miles, are the highest peaks. The middle section of the Appalachians is the Great Valley, which is really four valleys: the Central, Southern, East Tennessee, and Southwest Virginia Valleys, marked with bordering rugged ridges. On the west is the Cumberland Plateau, cut and carved by numerous streams, where the valleys are so narrow that in many places there is little more than room enough for the stream itself on the valley floor. Horace Kephart notes that United States topographers report that in Appalachia as a whole the mountain slopes occupy 90 percent of the total area and that 85 percent of the land has a steeper slope than one foot in five.[1]

As the pressure of population on the East Coast grew with the increasing migration from overseas, the search for westward-leading breaks in these mountains began. The first significant event was the discovery in 1750 of the Cumberland Gap, through which settlers poured in an ever increasing stream. By 1770 there were already settlers south of the Ohio River in Kentucky; in 1790, according to the first census, the total population of Southern Appalachia was 175,189, and over half of these resided in the territory that is now the state of Virginia. In 1818 the Cumberland turnpike was opened between Baltimore and the West, permitting an easier route down the Ohio, and the stream of English and Scottish settlers took this route rather than the more difficult and tortuous journey across the mountain ridges.

From the Cumberland turnpike families began to trickle into the mountains to settle. Those who came to the tight valleys were generally not the ones interested in settling down to a stable way of life and accumulating wealth and comfort and the benefits of a regulated society. Such folk either stayed on the coast or moved on to the river basins of the Ohio and the Mississippi or to the broad plains, where there were possibilities for more farmland, trade, business, and travel. The mountain settlers were more the perennial frontiersmen, interested in freedom from the restraints of law, order, and a differing culture. These were often the people who had been embittered by civilized life in England and Scotland and had come to these shores in rebellion against the very kind of society which they found already entrenched on the eastern shore. Indeed, even the place names along the eastern coast reflected a society continuous with that of the Old Country: New England, New York, Virginia. Some of the settlers, in fact, were released from

---

[1] *Our Southern Highlanders* (New York: Outing Publishing Co., 1913), p. 370.

debtor's prison on condition that they emigrate to the New World.

The early settlers included, too, many of those on the 'first frontier'—those land-hungry, self-sufficing farmers who were in opposition to many of the policies of the British crown and the seaboard regions, particularly on matters of land titles and Indian affairs."[2] They were determined to establish a life as free from contact with law and restraint as possible. In rebellion against a form of government that imposed its rule from the top, these people reverted to a system of private justice based on the personal relationships common to the clan. They thus developed a general ideology of leveling—a system that gave equal status to all and that recognized no authority other than the force of an individual. No hierarchy, authorities, or experts were allowed to form in this society; no pressure from outside was allowed to gain entrance.

The mountains of Appalachia provided the ideal setting for this kind of life, and into them these passionate lovers of freedom moved. Their difference in fundamental psychology from the other settlers who moved west began the accidents of history, environment, and circumstance which have led the southern highlander to a profound separation from his fellow countrymen in the rest of the nation.

At first, the broadest of the valleys of Appalachia were settled. The land was cleared of its virgin timber, log cabins were constructed, the fertile land was broken up and made productive. Game, berries, herbs, nuts, fruit, and lumber were in great abundance, and the local Indians were a source of information about living in such terrain. As on any frontier, life was hard and labor-saving devices were

[2] Carle C. Zimmerman and Richard E. DuWors, *Graphic Regional Sociology* (Cambridge, Mass.: Phillips Book Store, 1952), p. 40.

few; yet, in many ways, the people who settled here were rugged and ingenious. While they were not rich in goods, and had brought with them no outstanding skills in farming or hunting, life in the mountains was nevertheless good and there was little outside interference.

One wonders how long it was before the mountaineer began to realize, dimly at first, then ever more clearly, that there was a limit to the number of people these narrow valleys could support. Perhaps because they were not originally country people and had come largely in search of freedom from authority, these southern highlanders built their houses on the bottom lands and farmed the hillsides, in contrast to people in other mountainous areas who build houses on the slopes in order to farm the bottoms. Mountain families were large, and through natural increase more than any other way, the population grew, slowly but steadily. Because of the steep mountain barriers which effectually prevented any extensive travel beyond the local valley or area, sons and daughters tended to settle down close to parents, grandparents, and other kin. As the mountaineer's children left home to begin families of their own, however, they found that their parents already were cultivating the best ground for supporting crops. So they had to go farther upstream, where the valley was narrower and the fields smaller, some of them no more than ten feet wide. After a time families began to clear even the hillsides, farther and farther up. At first the hillside land was fertile enough, but contour farming as practiced in many mountainous areas was unknown here. The heavy rains of the region soon eroded these hillsides, filling the streams with mud and leaving gutted and infertile "perpendicular farms" where only the broom sedge could find root.

These "perpendicular farms" have been the source of

much humor, and mountain people enjoy the fun as much as anyone else. A mountain man I knew showed me a potato patch that rose at a steep angle right from his back door. It was difficult just to climb, let alone farm. I asked him whether it wasn't a hard job to farm a field like that. "Plantin's the hardest," he replied. "I have to lug all those 'taters clear to the top. But harvestin's easy. I take the bags and string up with me, fill the bags, tie 'em up and roll 'em down. When they're all dug, they're all layin' right at my door, right here."

The custom of settling close to kin has made each little valley the domain of a single family. It is not unusual today to find families with four generations living side by side in one narrow valley—brothers, sisters, aunts, uncles, nieces, nephews, and cousins—intermarrying to such an extent that in some fashion every person is related to every other. One often finds only two or three family names in a valley, and double first cousins are not uncommon. It frequently happens that a girl marries and does not even have to change her last name. One wonders how much this close intermarriage has affected the basic stock of the people of southern Appalachia.

Meanwhile, the settling of the nation went on apace. Turnpikes, then great railroads spanned and crisscrossed the continent, moving goods, people, and ideas from place to place—except in the mountains. Commerce, industry, education, and culture increased in the nation—but not in the mountains. There, time was standing still. The people spoke as they had always spoken; they preserved the old handicrafts and grubbed out a living in the old ways. They exchanged dried fruits, cured hams, ginseng, furs, and whiskey for cash and manufactured products. The gap between the culture of the towns and the mountains became both wide and deep. By the end of the nineteenth century, the mountaineers were a people apart, molded by the peculiar forces of the terrain, the pressure of economics, and the lack of contact with outsiders. "Conceive a shipload of emigrants cast away on some unknown island," writes Kephart, "far from the regular track of vessels, and left there for five or six generations, unaided and untroubled by the growth of civilization."[3] The mountains were proving to be not only a physical barrier but a social, cultural, economic, educational, and religious barrier as well.

The growing need for education, which was moving the nation toward ever better public schools and land-grant and private colleges, did not touch many a mountain family. The mountaineer derided education; it was thought to make one unfit for mountain life. In many parts of the hills, church groups established the first schools and carried them on, staffing and supporting them for years. Indeed, in many a mountain valley public education did not become a reality until the middle of the twentieth century. Many youths still consider the object of education to be "getting to sixteen years old so you can quit."

When the booming industry of the young nation spied the rich resources of the mountains, doors which should have opened began, instead, to close. First, it was the timber that was eyed, and representatives of the wood industries invaded the mountains, seeking to buy up the vast resources of virgin timber which covered every ridge and slope. The mountaineer, not used to bargaining in a money economy, quickly found himself at a disadvantage when he talked with the buyers. Many times he sold his timber for a pittance. He sold great trees up to eight feet in diameter for less than a dollar apiece, but there were so many that the total sum seemed to him a fortune. He was

[3] Kephart, p. 17.

hired to cut and get out the logs and to work in the saw-mills at a salary that was very low but enabled him to buy factory-made goods he had never had before, and he thought he was rich. It was not until some time afterward that he realized that he had been cheated.

As coal became a necessary fuel, men of industry again came to the southern mountains, this time to bargain for the coal deposits. Land companies were formed, and their representatives bought up vast tracts. Again the moun-taineer found himself at a disadvantage. Often he did not know that there was coal in the land he owned or had no knowledge of its extent. As with the timber, the moun-taineer did not know, even remotely, how much the coal was worth and would sell it for the going rate of fifty cents an acre; a few might get as much as five dollars an acre. The grandfather of a local barber sold a whole valley seven miles long, from ridge to ridge, including the virgin timber and seven seams of coal, a tract of several hun-dred acres, for $300 and a saddle horse. Frequently the land sold by the mountaineer would contain five or six minable seams of coal. Just one such seam, five feet thick, would produce over 5,000 tons an acre and, in today's prices, would be worth over $25,000 an acre.

The mountaineer would sign contracts he could not read, even bargaining away the rights to the land he wanted to keep for his farm and family. Only in later years was he to discover that he had hardly a scrap of right left to his homestead place. In conversation with people of the area I ran into one ingenious method by which land was pur-chased. Taking advantage of the chronic hard times and the scarcity of cash in the mountains, a local storekeeper who had learned there was coal in the area offered to let his customers pay for their groceries by signing over to him bit by bit their land or the mineral rights to it. The local families needed the food, clothing, and supplies provided by the store, and having no idea of the worth of their property, many of them agreed to the store keeper's proposition. Today this man's descendants own and control a vast amount of precious coal-bearing land.

Another method sometimes used by the land companies was the quit claim. Land agents would approach the unsuspecting mountaineer with the news that he would have to move off his land. The mountain man would protest that he owned the land and had a deed to prove it. Then the land agent would inform him that the company had a deed older than his and was ready to contest the issue in the courts. The mountaineer, not wishing an expensive court fight (an unknown and forbidding world to him), would accept a quit claim settlement in return for the "privilege" of continuing to live on the land. In this way the land company would get the mineral and timber rights (which it wanted) and the mountaineer would avoid a court battle and be allowed to live in peace (which was what he wanted).

Such fraud was not a part of every land transaction, of course, but trickery occurred all too often, and these instances are remembered with bitterness. For many mountaineers, the land companies are the real villains who are responsible for the past and present troubles in their lives. In *Night Comes to the Cumberlands,* Harry Caudill describes in detail the operations of the land companies.

The coal industry began to transform great sections of the mountains. Railroads and installations called "tipples" were built to handle the coal. Coal camps were built around the company store in many a remote hollow. The coal-camp houses were often slapped together in assembly-line fashion, all the same style and painted the same color. Row upon row they filled the bottoms and rose up the steep hillsides. Thus began the boom-and-bust coal economy, which alternately fed and starved, supported and broke down its people.

Is it any wonder that the people of Appalachia have, through the years developed as a people apart—and that their culture is different in many ways from the dominant middle class culture of America? Faced with so many unique hostilities of environment, heritage, and economics, the southern mountaineer has preserved a way of life all his own. "Why are they so foreign to present-day Americans that they innocently call all the rest of us foreigners?" asks Horace Kephart. "The answer lies on the map. They are creatures of environment, enmeshed in a labyrinth that has deflected and repelled the march of our nation for three hundred years."[4]

THE INROADS OF POVERTY

It is indeed difficult to point to a date or even a generation which can be labeled the "beginning of poverty" in the mountains. The early settlers were poor, but probably no more so than any pioneers just getting started in any section of our nation. And some persons in the region soon began to grow wealthy as farmers, commercial people, timbermen, or coal operators. Yet, as the wealth of America grew, the wealth of the mountains remained for the most part static.

The timber and coal belonged to outsiders who took them away to be used to create wealth for others in the form of finished products. Farms were too small to be profitable. More than a generation ago the industrial revolution hit agriculture, making it impossible for the mountain farmer to compete with the flatland farmers of the

[4] Kephart, pp. 18-19.

rest of the nation. The mountain farmers could neither afford nor use the labor-saving machinery which had so increased the efficiency of other American farms. Even a generation ago farming in Appalachia was far behind the rest of the nation. The 1930 census of agriculture showed that the Appalachian region contained the highest percentage of low-income farms in the nation. According to every meauring device the census used, the Appalachian farm was uneconomical. Some mountain farms returned less than $600 per year value of gross products, while the density of farm population was some 50 percent higher than that in the best farm areas of the Middle West, where yields were higher and the land better adapted to farming. The farmers of the Cumberland Plateau were found to be the lowest income group in United States agriculture.[5] Though some improvement in the agricultural economy has been made since 1930, particularly in favorable areas, agriculture in the region as a whole continues to be at best a marginal enterprise.

During the First World War, the coal fields boomed, pouring out their precious black fuel for the blast furnaces of the nation. When the war ended, so did the jobs of thousands of coal miners. Union strife began; attempts were made to organize the miners, and suffering increased as men were idle for months without pay.

The Great Depression of the early 1930s hit the coal fields with staggering force. A study of a number of coal-producing counties of Appalachia, where an average of half a million persons were on relief during the fiscal year 1934-35, concluded that 350,000 people should leave the area's agriculture and that 60,000 should leave mining. Theoretically, it was determined, some 640,000 persons,

[5] Rupert B. Vance, "The Region: A New Survey," in *The Southern Appalachian Region: A Survey*, ed. Thomas R. Ford (Lexington: University of Kentucky Press, 1962), p. 5.

27 percent of the area's population, should leave in order to bring the living standards up to the level of the United States at large.[6] According to federal criteria, at least half the population in some areas was eligible for relief. Many of those who managed to get on one of the welfare programs of the federal government found their way of life much improved, so low had been their income before.

As the American economy slowly lifted itself out of the doldrums of the thirties, Appalachia's economy continued to lag. Then the coal industry boomed again during the Second World War, as the steel mills gulped the fuel to make steel for armaments. Following the war, the clamor for consumer goods kept the steel mills running full blast, and the coal rolled out of the twisting valleys in long trainloads. The Korean conflict added the final spurt to the boom, although other factors began to affect the coal economy adversely.

Other fuels were beginning to cut into the market which coal had previously had to itself. Natural gas was piped to the industrial East from as far away as Texas. It was convenient to use, easily adaptable to automatic controls, and cheaper to transport than the bulky coal. Oil replaced coal for industrial heating and for train locomotives. For many years coal-burning steam engines pulled the coal trains out of the valley where I lived. In 1954, the very day after the last and largest mine closed its doors forever, it was a diesel that came up the valley to pick up the remaining cars and take them away, almost as if to say, "Go ahead and shut down your mines. Who needs coal?"

In order to compete with oil and gas, the coal industry quickly had to find ways to mine coal more cheaply, using fewer high-paid men. Automation came quickly; within ten years it had displaced nearly two-thirds of the men in

[6] Vance, p. 5.

the industry. By this means, the price of coal was kept down to a competitive figure, since the cost per ton at the mine has fluctuated little between 1940 and 1960 and the machines continue to produce as much as was mined before.

Often without a day's warning, men were cut off from their jobs. At one mine, which had worked steadily for forty years, the men returned from their annual vacation to find the place closed and their jobs gone. No warning had been given them before they left to spend their precious savings on recreation. At another mine, the men came to the lamp house the day before Thanksgiving to get their lamps for work underground and read on the bulletin board that, as of the last shift of the day, the mine would work no more. Hundreds of thousands of men found themselves with no jobs, no skills, little education, little or no experience living outside the mountains, and no desire to leave the only home they had ever known. The place-bound mountaineer found himself caught in poverty more severe than ever, at a time when more education, more training, and more skills were being called for by the American economy.

This last blow has been too great to overcome. Thousands of men whose only skill was no longer needed simply gave up. A study of those on welfare rolls in one mountain state has found that the shock of unemployability may so reduce a man's interest in work that within only a few years he becomes physically unemployable.

Thus has poverty deepened in both the farming areas and the mining counties. This is not to say that all of Appalachia has suffered. Many of the region's cities continue to grow and flourish, diversifying their economies with various industries. A number of thriving coal communities still go along at a high level of production. About these there is no reason to write, since they present no more problems than do similar prosperous areas anywhere. It is to the suffering parts, which include a high percentage of Appalachia's people, that my concern is mainly directed.

As the mines shut down, as the farms could no longer produce a living for those who worked them, as stores closed because of the loss of sales, men and families by the thousands began a flood of migration from the mountains to the cities of the North and East. Over the past decade, a hundred thousand or more persons a year have moved away from the mountains to Chicago, Columbus, Detroit, Cincinnati, and other metropolitan centers where at least the possibility of jobs has existed. Who were these people? Most often they were the young couples, with strength and ambitions for themselves and their children, who were not content with a marginal existence; they were the better-educated adults who could find in the cities the kind of employment that would enable them to live comfortably (often with the wife working, too); they were the leaders who had the skills that were useful in the cities —and would also have been useful in the mountains.

Who stayed behind? Storekeepers, teachers, and highly skilled coal miners who were still working, of course, but beyond these it was the poorly trained and poorly educated, who could find either no jobs or else such poor jobs that life in the cities would have had to be lived in the undesirable slums; the unambitious, who could tolerate a subsistence living at home; those above forty, who find it hard to be retrained and who are not wanted in the already overfull labor market; the aged, the sickly, and the retarded; and the psychologically immobile, who could not move away from the familiar, protective mountain culture. There are also some families who moved away and came back again, utterly discouraged and beaten. Their jobs "played out," and they had nothing saved to live on while they looked for other work. Some couldn't stand the pace of city life. In other instances, wives and children so hated the poorer section of the city, where they had to spend all day, that they threatened to leave if the husband's didn't "come back home" to the mountains. Appalachia has many such families who just couldn't make out in the cities and have come back to eke out the barest existence in the best way they can. Surely these folk add little to the morale of an already defeated population.

In these hard-hit areas of Appalachia, obviously, the culture of poverty becomes all the more entrenched, for many of those who could come nearest to doing something about the situation have moved to greener pastures. Because of the nature of the terrain, much of Appalachia is rural, and "from the viewpoint of the people themselves, the lack of metropolitan informed leadership is the greatest problem. Every other class and region in the United States has its intellectual leadership institutionalized in a metropolitan community, a number of universities, or a social institution. Not so the mountaineer. He simply has little or no understanding or information about the complexities of modern life. And he has lacked effective leadership."[7] Few mountain communities have the slightest expectation that their college-trained youth will ever come back to help them. Opportunities are too scarce. They simply move elsewhere, often out of the state.

The schools in these areas are left with a great percentage of content-retarded, sometimes less able children, and fewer resources to deal with them. They are left with a greater proportion of children from homes that do not value an education; these children become a drag on the achievement of the whole school system. As families leave,

[7] Zimmerman and DuWors, p. 46.

schoolrooms become empty, classes must double up to two and three grades per room, teachers become discouraged and leave for other states paying higher salaries. Businessmen have to close their establishments because of a lack of trade. Houses are boarded up; lawns grow up in weeds; towns disappear from the map or become ghost towns inhabited by a few indigent families or those who draw small checks—all adding to the feeling of despair and hopelessness that hangs over the area. Churches struggle along with fewer members to support them, fewer leaders, and decreasing morale. Doctors move away because they cannot make an adequate living, even though the need for medical care for the aging population may actually be increasing.

Competition increases between the businesses that are left, as the outlook becomes "if one of us has to close doors, let it not be me." The struggle for available jobs gets fiercer, and life is dominated by an attitude of "look out for yourself, and grab what you can as it comes along." At the time when cooperation is most needed, it is least likely to occur. Those whose philosophy has been a rugged independence in all things soon find themselves more than willing to put out both hands to receive anything that anyone offers. A whole segment of the region's people is on the way to being destroyed by forces too great and problems too long standing for them to cope with.

THE REDISCOVERY

For many years the Appalachian mountain region has been regarded as the "backwoods" area of our nation——never really known, not very often visited. Now, more than 300 years after it was first settled, this great land area, 600 miles long and nearly 250 miles across, touching

at least nine states and including eight million people, is
being rediscovered. Behind the stereotype of the "mountaineer," America is finding real people of flesh and blood:
genuine and often naive people who have been caught for
generations behind the wall of hills; people with brave
hearts and uncomplaining tongues; people whose an-
cestry goes back to the very early settlers of our nation,
who have yet to experience what it means to be living
in a land of opportunity and abundance; people who have
given thousands of their sons to fight bravely in the nation's
wars, yet who share little of the nation's life; people, to
top it all, who are among the nation's first victims of automation, the new power we do not yet know how to handle.
Within the past few years the area has come to the attention of many groups, private and governmental. The West
Virginia presidential primary of 1960 focused the national
eye on Appalachia. Out of this came an increased interest
in the problems of unemployment and poverty: books were
written, newspaper articles published, and studies made—
The Southern Appalachian Region: A Survey, sponsored
by the Ford Foundation, being among the finest of the
latter. Now, of course, we have the War on Poverty, with
such components as the Appalachian Recovery Act and
the Economic Opportunity Act.

Progress has come to many parts of Appalacina in the
past generation, and at an increasingly rapid pace. Many
cities in the area have witnessed industries moving in, new
colleges, hospitals, and health centers being built and used,
cultural advantages being developed and appreciated. Yet
as this has been happening, the rest of the nation has been
moving forward at an even greater pace. One wonders
whether Appalachia can be content with its one step forward while the rest of the nation has been taking two.
In the midst of pocket affluence in parts of Appalachia,

hundreds of thousands of families still live up the hollows and valleys untouched by it all.

No one will ever say that the problems of persistent poverty can be solved quickly in Appalachia. Almost fifty years ago now, Horace Kephart wrote that "the mountaineers of today are face to face with a mighty change . . . a new era dawns. Everywhere the highways of civilization are pushing into remote mountain fastnesses. . . . [T]he highlander, at last, is to be caught up in the current of human progress."[8] While changes have occurred in the half-century since Kephart wrote, nothing as dramatic as he envisioned has taken place, for the problems he described then still exist in major form today.

In *The Affluent Society*, John Kenneth Galbraith outlines a formidable battle plan to eliminate poverty. "The first and strategic step in an attack on poverty is to see that it is no longer self-perpetuating. This means insuring that the investment in children from families presently afflicted be as little below normal as possible. If the children of poor families have first-rate schools and school attendance is properly enforced; if the children, though badly fed at home, are well nourished at school; if the community has sound health services, and the physical well-being of the children is vigilantly watched; if there is opportunity for advanced education for those who qualify regardless of means; and if, especially in the case of urban communities, law and order are well enforced and recreation is adequate—then there is a very good chance that the children of the very poor will come to maturity without grave disadvantage."[9]

On the same page, however, Galbraith points to a problem. "Poverty is self-perpetuating," he says, "because the

---

[8] Kephart, pp. 376-77.
[9] (Boston: Houghton Mifflin Company, 1958), p. 330.

poorest communities are poorest in the services which would eliminate it." This is the situation in much of Appalachia. The "ifs" Galbraith mentions presuppose services which are practically nonexistent. Michael Harrington offers a gloomier prognosis: "It seems likely that the Appalachians will continue going down, that its lovely mountains and hills will house a culture of poverty and despair, and that it will become a reservation for the old, the apathetic, and the misfits."[10]

How to begin and where to start? How does one approach the problem of compartmentation—the environmental problem created by the valleys of Appalachia? How does one break down the extreme isolation that so many families choose as their way of life and pass on to their children? Education is an answer, yes, but what can be done with families who have lived with generations of antipathy to schooling? How can we reach a people with twentieth-century education who still live by seventeenth-century social and economic codes? Plans may well be made to improve the educational level of the young, yet for what? To move elsewhere for jobs and life, leaving the valleys still bereft? And, further, how does one bring first-rate, modern education through school systems so beleaguered by lack of funds and political maneuvering that new well-trained personnel from outside the area are not wanted?

The economic situation is equally unpromising. Lack of transportation for goods, distance from sizable markets, inadequate water and sewerage systems, substandard housing and schools, little available land, and an untrained labor supply—how many more economic strikes could a region have against it?

[10] *The Other American: Poverty in the United States* (New York: Macmillan Company, 1962), p. 43.

To these problems of education and economics we must add the poor or nonexistent private and public health systems that plague many a mountain county. Poor health services simply perpetuate the plight of the people, piling more burdens on an already overburdened populace. "Lack of education and information, of facility in reading and writing, of interest in relatively abstract things: habits of submission, feelings of inferiority, low income, absorption with the problem of mere survival—all these factors continually influence one another, so that we cannot attempt to show where one begins and the other ends."[11] And the nature of Appalachia's problems is compounded by the fact that many people who live in the midst of the problems do not even admit that the problems exist, do not even realize how fast the country is moving away from the mountain type of economy, education, and outlook.

[11] Genevieve Knupfer, "Portrait of The Underdog," in *Class, Status and Power: A Reader in Social Stratification,* ed. Reinhard Bendix and Seymour Martin Lipset (Glencoe, Ill.: The Free Press, 1953), p. 256.

3.

Introducing the Mountaineer

A MERICAN society has loved the caricaturization of the cowboy, and his ways have found entrance into the dreams and play of many an American child. There is something romantic and wholesome about the cowboy. The "western" image has a significant role in American entertainment, business, and even politics and religion. (Note the ten-gallon hat and boots that many Westerners still wear, and the evangelistic impact made by Roy Rogers and Dale Evans.)

The mountaineer, on the other hand, has become an object of amusement and scorn. Who has not been confronted by a picture of the bare-footed man in ill-fitting homemade clothes, with a jug over one shoulder and his rifle in hand? His supposed affinity for "corn in the bottle," which he makes illegally, his shiftlessness, and his outmoded speech are staples of this image.

Why is it that we regard one segment of our population as heroic, while another is, at best, pathetically amusing? Is it because the cowboy was successful in meeting the challenge of his environment before he became the victim of a changing economy, whereas the mountaineer, for generations cut off from the main stream of American life, seeks to meet the modern age with the same old-fashioned weapons? Or is it because the cowboy represents a frontier that, being gone, can be romanticized, while the mountaineer still lives on his frontier without having conquered it?

The cowboy was able to accept the changing economy, the fenced range, moving from horse travel to truck, jeep, and even plane and helicopter. Each change that came to the mountaineer, however, was a threat, or served to embitter or further impoverish him.

While the cowboy had what may be described as an "open door" culture, which presented him with opportunity for progress, the mountaineer had a "closed door" culture, which denied him the chance of advancement. How much his situation resembles the hero's in Kafka's *The Trial*: "The door keeper perceives that the man is at the end of his strength and that his hearing is failing, so he bellows in his ear: 'No one but you could gain admittance through this door, since the door was intended only for you. I am now going to shut it.' "[1]

It should not be surprising to find that the mountaineer has been molded in certain peculiar ways and that his culture has developed along lines that would allow him to bear up under the crushing loads he had put upon him. Just as the rubbing shoe, unknown to the wearer, begins to put calluses on the foot, changing its contour, so the mountaineer has had calluses rubbed on his mind and soul, worn there by the constant brushes of his life against a tight environment and an economy that denied him room to develop freely.[2]

INDIVIDUALISM

A fierce independence was part of the heritage which the settlers brought with them to the region; it proved to

[1] Franz Kafka, *The Trial*, trans. Willa and Edwin Muir (New York: Alfred A. Knopf, 1945), pp. 270-71.

[2] In this chapter I have made use of some of the categories and findings of Thomas R. Ford's chapter, "The Passing of Provincialism," in *The Southern Appalachian Region: A Survey* (Lexington: University of Kentucky Press, 1962), pp. 9-34.

be an absolutely essential trait. Since the hollow where a family lived was separated from the hollows where their neighbors lived, transportation and communication between them was infrequent. Each household lived its own separate life. Each man became his own provider, his own law and protector, his family's agent to the outside world, its doctor and dentist and even teacher for the children, since no one else could be counted on to provide these services. Hence the mountaineer came to. admire the man who was most independent, both economically and socially. "Here, then, is a key to much that is puzzling in highland character. In the beginning, isolation was forced upon the mountaineers; they accepted it as inevitable and bore it with stoical fortitude until in time they came to love solitude for its own sake and to find compensations in it for lack of society."[3]

Some activities in mountain life were cooperative—the corn husking, the cabin raising, the quilting parties, the building of a church—but these were the exception rather than the rule. I know of many mountain communities where not a single sustained cooperative activity takes place to this day. Each family makes its own way, even though it is evident that there are needs requiring the strength and assistance of a group working together; the pattern of each depending upon his own talent, strength, and resourcefulness is too deeply ingrained.

Here, through the generations, a subtle but significant change took place. Independence has become individualism, which includes independence but has a different direction. On the one hand, independence means simply a certain autonomy of person in the way one lives and thinks and acts. A man with independence may well work

[3] Horace Kephart, *Our Southern Highlanders* (New York: Outing Publishing Co., 1913), p. 306.

in his own way for a cooperative and common good. Surely many of the great leaders of the world have been independent thinkers and self-reliant doers. This is a quality we would not wish to lose from our common life. The independent and self-reliant spirit is a valuable asset for any people.

Individualism, on the other hand, has a self-directed quality in it: a man works, perhaps in independent ways, with his own gain or well-being in mind. It is to this quality of individualism that the mountaineer's independence has come. All that he does has the self and its concerns at heart. He is self-centeredly independent, so that even if he does join a group (a union, a PTA, or even a church) his intention, however unconscious, is that the organization shall serve his own personal interests and needs. If it does not, even though it may be serving a worthwhile goal, he will not continue in the group. He does not conceive of the "public good" except as it coincides with his own "private good."

Accordingly, public welfare was not rejected by mountain people but was widely welcomed when it first came in the form of the New Deal during the 1930s. A man could accept a check and go on living up the hollows as he had always done, for few claims were put upon him in return for this assistance. It became simply another way of earning a living —the government was serving individualism's need in a wonderful way. For some, the matter of getting a small check became a real challenge, and ingenious ways of qualifying were devised—another demonstration of self-reliance gone to extremes!

To a question posed in Ford's essay, "Do you think the present relief and welfare program is a good thing?" six out of seven respondents agreed that it is, and two out of three indicated there is no stigma attached to a family's being on relief. When the question was asked, "Do you think Federal aid to local areas makes the people less self-reliant?" 49 percent said they thought it does, while only 32 percent said they thought it does not.[4] This bears out the fact that a good many mountaineers do not value self-reliance as firmly as might be supposed, since they are willing to receive public assistance. It is their trait of individualism that is served.

This independence-turned-individualism, a corruption of the virtue which was once the foundation stone of the mountain man's way of life, now proves to be a great stumbling block to his finding a place in our increasingly complex and cooperative society. A man cannot "go it alone" in our modern age. We have found, for example, that many a mountain family living up a hollow is reluctant to take advantage of sewing, cooking, or farming classes offered in central places, even though they would admittedly profit greatly from them. The way to help these families without violating their individualistic needs is to take the assistance to one family, then to another. Obviously, this requires a great deal of manpower and time and the frustrating task of repeating the same lesson or help over and over. But it puts the burden of responsibility for the program on the offerer and frees the family from responsibility for failure. They didn't ask for the help—it was offered, and they simply accepted.

In the past generation, the spirit of cooperation has been growing among mountain people, although the individualism of the past is still strong enough to hold back a wholehearted cooperative effort. Yet, as increasing numbers of persons endorse the work of labor unions, PTA's, 4-H clubs, and community improvement programs—even if such endorsements are only words—a changing attitude becomes evident.

One interesting corollary in the opinion section of *The*

4 Ford, pp. 13-14.

Southern Appalachian Region is that, although most people were interested in cooperative programs, they were not willing to support them by local taxes.[5] Here again the mountaineer's individualism comes to the fore. He does not see government as a "we," a cooperative extension of himself, but only as a "they." He wants, and expects, this government to care for him, but he does not want to have to pay for it. But, as the survey notes, this is not a trait peculiar to mountain people!

TRADITIONALISM

A second significant trait of the mountain man is traditionalism. He is bound to the past in an amazing way: "their adherence to old ways is stubborn, sullen, and perverse to a degree that others cannot comprehend."[6] While much of American culture has faced so many changes within the last hundred years as to leave many people virtually rootless, mountain life, as it has continued in its more or less static way, has preserved the old traditions and ideas, even encouraged them. As long ago as 1899 the people were characterized as "contemporary ancestors."[7]

Let me describe this quality in two ways, using two different sets of word parallels, each of which sets a slightly different stage for our thinking.

The first of these descriptions I found in an exhibition of old mountain farm buildings and equipment in the Great Smoky Mountains National Park. Here the words used to differentiate the outlook of mountain subculture from the middle class culture of America outside the region were "regressive" and "progressive."

[5] Ford, p. 15.
[6] Kephart, p. 23.
[7] William G. Frost, "Our Contemporary Ancestors in the Southern Mountains," *Atlantic Monthly*, LXXXIII (March 1899), pp. 311-19.

Most Americans are "progressive"; that is, we look ahead with at least some expectation of joy and encouragement. We have lived a good portion of our lives in times which have led us to believe that next year things will be better. Tomorrow will bring new opportunities, new experiences. We expect our children to have more than we have of the things that make life enjoyable and comfortable. They will have better education, better jobs. We look ahead to tomorrow with pleasant anticipation.

The mountain man, however, has a "regressive" outlook, for he does not look forward to tomorrow with pleasant anticipation. For generations, his life has been hard and uncertain. The sharp limit to the amount of land available for supporting his increasing family; its low productivity, because of his unscientific methods; the uncertainty of life in the mines, where he was never sure that he would come out of the hole alive after the shift; the insecurity of life tomorrow if the breadwinner were maimed or killed in the mines, and the family was forced to move; the chance of the cutoff slip coming without warning—all were factors which led the mountaineer to look, not ahead to an uncertain tomorrow, but backward to a yesterday which was remembered, perhaps nostalgically, as being happier than today. Yesterday the family was still together. Children were still at home instead of away working. Parents were still alive. The old homestead was still standing. The old values held firm.

Much of mountain music is nostalgic and melancholy, even to the forms of harmony, which give it a certain feeling of loneliness and yearning. Mountain ballads often refer to friends, family, or situations of a time now past. Much of mountain literature is backward looking. Folk stories paint the picture of the hero going back home, either to find the old security again around the fireplace or front porch, or else to find it gone, while memories flood in. Much of mountain talk and gossip is backward oriented: how things used to be, how much better things were, what fun people used to have, how "everybody" went to church then—as if the "good old days" held the only joy. Too often the tomorrows of life have held only sorrows, fears, frustrations, or disappointments. The outlook of the mountain man's culture is "regressive."

The second set of word parallels that help to explain the meaning of traditionalism consists of the phrases "existence oriented" and "improvement oriented." Middle class America tends to be improvement oriented; its people are not satisfied with mere survival at the level on which they find themselves. They want things to be better—a more modern-looking mailbox, a newer car, a better house, a vacation house by the lake, more education or cultural advantages, a better community. The middle class American has a general desire for excellence in everything about his life. He is always striving for something—better and more. Improvement is a great motivating force in his life.

The existence oriented society, on the other hand, is geared toward achieving only the very basic goods needed for survival—food, clothing, shelter, and minimum of comfort. The secondary goals of beauty, excellence, refinement, "the good life"—these are not considered. This description characterizes much of mountain life. Even when a coal miner is enjoying a good income because of a long period of steady work, his house—which he may own—may show no sign of improvement, and his cultural investment for himself and his family may show little change. He is contented with just getting along. Satisfied when his survival goals are achieved, the mountaineer seldom looks beyond them. He is, for instance, a very poor contributor to fund drives for community betterment programs. He simply does not see the need for, or the value of, supporting such improvements with his money (or his energy). The mountaineer insists that his taxes be kept unbelievably low, even while he complains that his schools, roads, and public health and welfare services are incredibly inadequate. For example, several kindergartens were being sponsored by our parishes in order to prepare children for the first grade. In one of these, the parents would not pay more than five dollars a semester for each child, even though expenses were much higher than this and most of the families could pay more. They had been able to get along all these years without this program, so why was it necessary to spend much for it now?

Mountain youth, are the least traditionalistic; yet the tendency is still prevalent, even in them. They are not ready and eager for new ideas and new experiences, but cling closely to the forms and clichés that are the bulwarks of the older generation. This existence orientation makes the whole society very conservative in every aspect of its life, almost passive in accepting the status quo, for things are all right as they are and change seems always for the worse. Even for the youth, the tomorrows are looked upon not with a sense of challenge and adventure but with suspicion and some trepidation. For instance, a visiting youth group tried through private conversations to discover the aims of the local young people. They found that the local youths held few realistic hopes or ambitions and were seldom able to articulate goals, and were even reluctant to talk about the future.

Middle class children are brought up expecting that they will succeed, and they are helped by their parents to move toward success, subordinating their present wishes in favor of long-range plans. Mountain children, however, have had very few contacts with successful adults, and their families have been unable to help them achieve a success in the outside world about which they know little.

FATALISM

Within the folk culture, fatalism has joined hands with traditionalism to give the mountaineer's outlook a somewhat different cast from that of people in other rural societies in which traditionalism is also a characteristic. It is not to be supposed that the qualities of fatalism and traditionalism were wedded in the early pioneers of the area. No doubt these families had as high hopes as any pioneers in other parts of our nation. On the great plains, the homesteaders met with some degree of success in achieving wealth, comfort, and security. In the mountains, however, nature did not yield; instead, the harshness of the land overcame the man. His confidence in himself was slowly but surely undermined. From this grew a fatalistic attitude, which allowed him to live without the guilty feeling that he himself was to blame for his lot and assured him that this way of life was fundamentally right even when he was discouraged by it.

While traditionalism can thwart the planners and molders of industry, education, and society in general, fatalism can so stultify a people that passive resignation becomes the approved norm, and acceptance of undesirable conditions becomes the way of life. There is no rebellion, little questioning, little complaining. Observing this, a reporter who came to the area to write a story about what unemployment was doing to families remarked, "Nobody yells about the situation, do they?" She added, "But I guess there is nobody to yell to who could do any good, anyway, is there?" Precisely!

The fatalism of mountain people has a religious quality to it: "If that's the way God wants it, I reckon that's the way it'll be. We just have to take what the Lord sends us. He knows best." In *The Southern Appalachian Region* these ideas were expressed as "Nowadays a person has to live pretty much for today and let tomorrow take care of itself" and "No matter how much or how little you take care of yourself, you are going to die when your alloted time is up"— statements to which a high percentage of persons responded in the affirmative.[8] I have heard many a coal miner express the latter thought as his security for going into the mines day after day.

Being poor is declared to be a holier state than being rich. This justification of a deprived condition is emotional rather than intellectual. To argue against it puts one in the position of being against holiness. Many a mountain preacher is greeted with hearty "amens" when he speaks on the theme of the beatitude, "blessed are you poor," or the words of Jesus, "Woe to you that are rich." It is even said that the way you can tell a good man from a bad one is to see how poor he is: the poorer the man, the healthier the soul; "the heavier the load, the brighter the crown."

This fatalistic outlook has been a kind of buffer against disappointment. Mountaineers are never very optimistic about anything. Hopes are couched in tentative terms. It is, indeed, a subdued society. Even among little children there is often a passive, repressed quality instead of the spontaneous laughter and freedom so common to children elsewhere in our society. In talking with young people, whom one would expect to be idealistic and ready to tackle the world, one often finds that their attitudes toward the future and their hopes for success are those of unsuccessful adults. Sometimes it seems that they are beaten before they ever have a chance to try.

There are some illogical conflicts in this fatalism as it

8 Ford, p. 20.

is worked out in the life of the people. Doctors are seen when sickness occurs, even though the statement is made that when your time is up, there is nothing you can do. In the opinion poll of *The Southern Appalachian Region* parents expressed the belief that children of today can look forward to a good future. While fatalism claims that you can do little to improve your lot in life, the response to the question whether God is more pleased when we try to get ahead or when we are satisfied with things the way they are indicated that socioeconomic status determines one's answer. Those in the upper income group were mostly sure that God was satisfied when people tried to get ahead, whereas the lower income group indicated that they thought God was more pleased when people were satisfied with their lot.[9] Though the general conversational assumptions of people in the mountains are fatalistic, it is no surprise that those who have the least to show for their work will follow the philosophy most consistently.

The opinion survey in *The Southern Appalachian Region* indicates that both fatalism and traditionalism are receding. Questions dealing with the aspirations of parents for their children revealed that parents are interested in their children's going on to school, taking opportunities open to them, seeking white-collar jobs, even moving away from home where jobs and hopes are scarce. Numbers of respondents indicated by their answers that they believe that people do have a significant part in making a successful life. Hard work and training were said to be very important in making a good living. It was interesting that the proportion of respondents who gave primary importance to the necessity of hard work in making a successful life declined steadily from the oldest to the youngest group. Apparently the old-timers still think that hard work is one of the main ingredients in

9 Ford, pp. 20-21.

the successful life—a most amazing conclusion in the light of the tremendous amounts of hard work they have expended for so little material return.

SEEKERS OF ACTION

A set of words describing another characteristic difference between the mountain man and his middle class counterpart is "action seeking" and "routine seeking."[10] If we were to draw a scale of behavior with action seeking at one extreme and routine seeking at the other, we would all fit somewhere in the middle; at different times and in different situations we would move toward one end or the other. The traits cannot be thought of as precisely measurable, so that we can each be pinpointed on the scale, but only describe a tendency.

The middle class man tends to be a routine seeker, finding the satisfaction and pleasure of his life in the routine of every day. It is from this routine that life gets its real meaning and through it that the work of life is done. The housewife finds a sense of security in washing on Monday, ironing on Tuesday, cleaning on Wednesday, and so on the rest of the week. A certain style of eating is developed, including particular kinds and quantities of food for breakfast, lunch, and dinner. Routine-seeking families have traditional celebrations on holidays or special days of the year. Christmas is celebrated in a certain way; the Fourth of July has a certain kind of picnic. The same persons are given gifts or sent cards on special days. The day, the week, the year have a regular rhythm, and if it is disturbed a crisis of more or less severity results. We come to enjoy having certain hours to get up; certain times to get to work; certain friends to meet

---

[10] This pair of contrasting phrases is taken from Herbert J. Gans, *The Urban Villagers* (New York: Free Press of Glencoe, 1962), pp. 28-31.

in the car pool or at work or lunch; certain clubs to attend on various nights. It is in the routine of life that the daily round makes the most sense and gives the most pleasure.

The routine seeker makes a constant effort to establish a stable way of life socially, economically, and emotionally. A regular, secure job is a necessity and is the object of search. The routine seeker is likely to attend church on a regular basis and participate in the on-going work it has to do. He is likely to join clubs that have long-range plans or that in the long run have values that are those he wants to uphold but that are not easily taught or achieved, such as citizenship or integrity or faithfulness to ideals. He saves money, looking forward not only to tomorrow, to the purchase of a cottage or a boat, but years ahead to the education of his children. He is content to live for years to build himself into a community in such a way that he will be respected. There is a highly regular and recurring schedule of behavior patterns, which is not in the least burdensome. Rather, it is sought and planned, for in this schedule his work is done, his satisfaction is found, his goals are achieved.

The action seeker is at the other end of the scale response. For him, life is episodic. During the routines he cannot escape, he usually just exists, waiting for the next episode of action that will provide the real meat of life. The routines are only endured; the satisfactions of life are found in action—those intermittent times of thrills, challenge, and excitement. The action seeker may well work all week long at a very routine job, but in this he finds little satisfaction. He is waiting for the weekend drinking bout, the card game, the hunting or fishing expedition, the horse or automobile race. His jobs are often the unstable ones, or those offering excitement or change.

Since educational pursuits are routine, the action seeker tends to reject them, although he may stick with them in order to participate in the sports activities of the school. He tends not to be a churchgoer, since church is a routine. On occasion, however, he may attend tent meetings and revivals, but such attendance really bears out his need for action. He is an impulsive spender, often wasting money that he could well use on necessities for his family; perhaps he buys a very expensive TV set or refrigerator just to satisfy his whim of the moment, his need to act. He saves little for a rainy day, or for the education of his children, or for projected goals in the future.

In his response to the life of every day, the mountaineer is an "action seeker." He does not wish to commit himself in advance to a routine meeting because something of an action nature, which he would greatly prefer, may come up at the last minute—a most frustrating trait to the calendar-minded middle class worker in the area. A meeting of some importance, planned weeks ahead, is spoiled because a key man is sidetracked: a friend who needs help in tearing down his old car has dropped in. The very night before a meeting you may check with every person who has tentatively agreed to go, but you never know how many are really going until they are in the car and on the way. It is difficult to sign young people up ahead of time for summer camp—"something might come up."

I gained an interesting insight into this aspect of mountain life during the painting of a country church. Many men in the community were unemployed, and we felt that if those who were working bought the paint, the others could put it on. After we bought the paint, we tried to line up volunteers. Not one man would commit himself: "I can't promise you nothin'. Somethin' might come up." One of the men in the congregation, instinctively understanding this psychology, suggested that we have the paint, brushes, and

ladders ready in front of the church one morning; as the men
went by on their way to the post office and general store, he
said, we could ask them whether they could paint for a
couple of hours that very day. Their response was remarkable. Many of the men painted all day every day until the
job was finished—men who beforehand would not agree to
being "signed up" for a single day. More than twenty men
helped with the job, the most who had worked together on
a project in that community within the memory of anyone
still living there.

In one church I suggested that at each service we have
a calendar with a printed order of worship. There was deep
emotional resistance to this idea. The people, though knowing fairly accurately beforehand the usual order of worship,
did not want to see at a glance what was to happen. They
wanted to retain the possibility of unknown action.

Coal mining is action. The dangers involved, the constant
movement of the job into ever new areas of work as the
coal is mined out, even the walkout and the strike—all lend
an excitement to the work that is anything but routine. Many
a coal miner will leave a steady, routine factory job in the
city any time to take a job back in the mines.

Women of the mountains can be much better counted on
to support the regular continuing activities of the church
and community groups. In all societies, women tend to be
farther along the scale toward routine seeking than men.

There is, of course, some of the routine seeker and some
of the action seeker in all of us. No one fits completely at
either extreme, but I believe the whole matter needs careful consideration by those middle and professional class
people who are working in the mountains. There are few
more frustrating and discouraging tasks than trying to
operate in routine ways in an action-seeking society.

THE PSYCHOLOGY OF FEAR

"Another characteristic outstanding among the mountain people is their fearlessness. Either they do not sense danger, or they are indifferent to it."[11] This is true of mountain people in response to some immediate and recognizable danger—a flash flood, a fire, or an accident. Men have related to me many admirable responses to danger in the mines or in the woods. The history of the area is full of illustrations of brave actions by the freedom-loving mountaineer.

In daily life, however, mountain society is filled with apprehension. Beneath his stoical manner, the slow-moving, apparently peaceful, self-assured mountain man or woman may well be the victim of intense anxieties. It is not uncommon even for young people in their early twenties to have bleeding ulcers. The simple request to speak a word or lead a meeting in public will strike debilitating fear into the hearts of most mountain folk.

Children are made to obey through fear: "I'll get the law after you, if you don't mind." When a stranger visits in the home, the children cling closely to their parents or hide behind them. I have heard parents say to their preschool children, as I called in their homes, "That man'll get you if you aren't good," or "I'll give you away to that man if you don't behave. He'll take you away with him." More adults fear "haunts," or ghosts, and graveyards than will readily admit it.

To the outsider, the mountain family is apparently close knit, which would seem to lend security to mountain life. In some respects, this is true. The members of a family, however, are bound to one another by ties of emotional

11 W. D. Weatherford and Earl D. C. Brewer, *Life and Religion in Southern Appalachia* (New York: Friendship Press, 1962), p. 10.

dependence which tend to increase insecurity. In a sense, the family is not so much a mutually supporting group, in which each member gives himself for the others, as it is a group in which each member demands support from the others. I have known young people who have expressed almost a hatred of home but could not be away from "Mommy" and "Daddy" for a weekend without becoming homesick.

Since one's security depends upon the approval of others in the family, there is always a fear of being misunderstood, and hence rejected, by the group upon whom one depends. In consequence, people go to great pains to avoid being misunderstood or creating hard feelings within the family. Of course, when one is expecting misunderstandings and hurt feelings, they very often occur. Chance remarks, made unthinkingly or in jest in the ordinary give-and-take of life, may be understood wrongly and recalled years afterward. There is a curious ambivalence in family relationships. On the one hand, members are dependent upon one another for security; on the other, they are suspicious of each other's intentions. One's rights are jealously guarded from encroachment by any of the others.

The occasion of the funeral is a case in point. I have seen undertakers at the very limit of their wits trying to get the family to decide on details. All the relatives must be consulted, and no one can be called upon to make decisions for the group, since there is a great fear of being misunderstood by the others or of slighting some of them. When the immediate family is willing to come to a decision, it is with an eye to what the larger family, and even the community, thinks. No one must be given cause for complaint or criticism.

Another example of the stresses of uncertainty in mountain families can be seen in the arrangements made about heirship land. In Appalachia great quantities of such land have been left by fathers and grandfathers to their children, who now hold the property jointly. Those who want the land for themselves cannot buy it from the others, who do not want it but don't want to see anybody else in the family have it. Thus it is passed down to each generation's children, the ownership being spread thinner and thinner while the land and buildings stand unused. In one example of such heirship property, a son who had to leave his rented house decided to move into the one-time parental dwelling, which had stood empty for years because the family could not decide who should have it or how it should be used or divided. When the son asked the others in the family whether he could move in, they would tell him neither yes nor no. He decided to move in anyway, and began to clean out the house. Immediately the house was set afire, and it burned to the ground—thus being removed from consideration.

Decision making of any kind is a difficult matter. In meetings, no one wants to state his mind or offer a motion unless he is confident that such action represents the consensus of the group. Opinions must be drawn forth piecemeal, with various members of the group contributing. In this manner stronger and stronger opinions may be expressed. If substantial disagreement should develop, factions immediately form. In any group where people mean to be on their best behavior, no vote can be taken unless the group is in agreement. No one will vote.

Never having been taught to face and overcome difficulties, but instead to retreat and "keep out of it," mountain people often have no confidence in their abilities. "I can't do that" is their common reaction on being asked to do something new, whether it be serving on a committee, being treasurer of a group, or taking part in a meeting. This response is not simply a case of extreme modesty, a man confessing that maybe there are others more able than himself, but expresses a deep fear of failure and consequent inferiority. Even young people often show this fear in fairly trivial matters.

One time the youth of the church planned a fund-raising dinner for the community. The girls were to serve and clear the tables. A brief training session was necessary for them, since none had ever done this kind of thing before, at least not outside of their own homes. As the rudiments of serving were being explained to them, one of the girls, a senior high student, broke down in tears because she was terribly afraid of doing something wrong.

There is great reluctance to speak with any one personally about a matter on which there may be a difference of opinion. Neighbors, at odds over the placement of a fence, will not face each other and talk through the matter, but will call the "law" to settle it for them. Few want to "meddle" in anybody else's business or offer advice.

As a newcomer to the area, I felt that the dirt road leading to the church property could be greatly improved by filling it in with slate, a mine refuse which the coal company would gladly haul for us and dump on the road. Presenting this to a committee, I met with no response beyond vaguely evasive mumbles. I went ahead with the project, only to find that at the first rain the slate crumbled into a greasy mess that made driving or walking hazardous. We had to hire a bulldozer to scrape it off. Only at the point of my realizing the error did the committee come forward with the fact that they had known all along what would happen. They had said nothing because they were afraid I would think they were opposing me.

Mountain people are indeed reared in a society of the "known," a rural environment providing little stimulation or opportunity, and thus acquire neither the attitude of mind nor the few skills needed for meeting new and different situations. There are few broadening experiences available to them—few simple experiences, like sitting with people you don't know on a bus, asking for change from a busdriver, doing business with strangers in stores or supermarkets, meeting and playing with strange children in the park. Though these are not usually thought of as social learning experiences, they actually are, for they teach people to be more competent and secure in new situations and more able to take in stride whatever comes along. Because mountain youths are surrounded by a culture that contains only what is known, they are often extremely reluctant and afraid to attempt any unfamiliar experience.

For example, a group of men from our area were being housed in a YMCA in a city where the church was seeking to relocate them. One night a member of the group stopped in the lobby for a candy bar while the others went on up to their rooms. Following along afterwards, he entered the automatic elevator, which had always been operated by someone else in the group. Finding himself alone with the doors closed, he panicked. He yelled and screamed and beat on the sides of the elevator until someone on the outside punched the button, opening the doors for him. He was so shaken by this experience that the next day he boarded a bus for home. There are no doubt many people who are still suspicious of these automatic devices; yet here was a young man in his early thirties who was so overwhelmed in this new situation that he could not handle his fear.

Such fear is not surprising, for mountain life has traditionally been insecure. This is true economically, for the mountaineer has never been financially secure either on his small farm or in the mines. This is true medically, for the mountaineer has not often shared the advantages of modern medicine. This is true religiously, for even his faith has been a fear-motivated one.

The very permissive and indulgent child-rearing practices of the mountain family also create insecurity, for children are trained to believe that their desires are paramount. Yet every child knows he is not capable of making decisions for himself, and he needs to find a security in parents who do know. The mountain child is made to depend upon his own choices very early in his life, thus building an insecurity into him almost from the start.

Because the mountaineer's security is dependent upon his relationships with those in his family and reference group (see Chapter 4), he must always rely on someone else. His security is not based within himself, on his own abilities and talents. Thus he can never be sure of himself as a person in his own right.

It is difficult and useless, perhaps, to try to name all the fears of the mountaineer, for apprehension pervades his whole life. One does not have to live long in the mountains to see that this anxiety affects persons of all ages, eating away at the relationships of person with person, even within families, at self-confidence, happiness, and health. The mountaineer lacks a confident sense of who he is and where he is going; instead, one finds a reluctant and anxious person who seems to ask for defeat by his very reluctance and uncertainty. Everybody who works in the mountains should be aware of this anxiety and its ramifications, for it determines in great measure the working of the group process as well as the kind and quality of response that can be expected from mountain people.

PERSON ORIENTATION

I have found Herbert Gans's concepts of person orientation and object orientation very helpful in my characterization of Southern mountain society.¹² Again, these words, of course, do not describe totally opposite patterns of behavior; seldom, if ever, would one expect to find any person whose behavior could be adequately described by either of these phrases. Rather, they are poles of behavior, between which we all operate, some of us more toward one pole than another, and individuals often shift on the scale in different situations.

These two poles of behavior are described by Gans in terms of their differences in aspirations. The object-oriented person strives toward a goal or object outside himself. This can be a moral object, a principle; a material object, such as a level of income or bank account; a cultural object, such as a particular style of life; a social object, such as a vocation or status in life; or an educational object, such as a college degree. The object-oriented person puts these objects, which are outside himself, as his goals; everything else is subordinated to these. If the persons in his family or among his friends do not share his hopes and labors for these goals, he will leave them to find persons who do share them. If the community in which he lives stands in his way or fails to provide whatever is needed toward the achieving of these object goals, he moves away to another place. In each case, the object toward which he strives can be conceptualized in a deliberate manner.

The person-oriented individual also strives, but not for objects. His concern is to be a person within the group. He wants to be liked, accepted, and noticed, and he will respond in kind to such attention. He is reluctant to separate himself from any group in which he finds this acceptance. His life goals are always achieved in relation to other persons and are a product of participation in the group. Without such a group, the goals cannot be achieved. While

¹² Gans, pp. 89 ff.

the object-oriented individual will either join or leave a group in order to achieve his goal, the person-oriented individual can find what he is seeking only within the group. For the object-oriented individual, ideas are central—something "out there," beyond the person himself. For the person-oriented individual, social relationships are central—something within and very personal, a security of acceptance, which can be found only within the group.

The more I live with these concepts, the more convinced I am that these poles tend to develop in particular kinds of situations. The object-oriented individual tends to develop in an "open door" society, where there is at least the possibility of achievement beyond the self—the possibility of advancement in the job or of changing jobs to suit the person's talents; the possibility of more education; the possibility of a gradual climb up the ladder of security or status. In "closed door" societies (and this can be in agrarian societies in America or anywhere in the world, in the Southern mountains or any inner city, or in static cultures everywhere), where the possibilities of advancement and achievement tend to be very limited, individuals, in order to find some fulfillment in life, center their aspirations on interpersonal relationships. There is little else that can be done, except by a few talented or strong persons who are able to move out toward object goals. In other words, a society which tends to limit the possibilities of freely achieving object goals inevitably forces people back into themselves to find the rewards of life. It is the only avenue left to them.

Object-oriented individuals see person-oriented individuals as having no goals, as lacking ambition to "make something of themselves," as seeking only the pleasures of the moment. Person-oriented individuals, however, see their counterparts as calculating, without heart, manipulators for personal gain (which does not really matter anyway), as unable to enjoy life because they are so caught up in striving. Each is at least partly wrong about the other: person-oriented individuals do have aspirations and ambitions, but these have to do with their relationships with other persons within the culture. Object-oriented individuals, on the other hand, do have personal relationships and develop ties of friendship, although these are usually sought in a much more deliberate way and enjoyment of life is found in the achievement of the object goals.

These designations, however, do not make it possible to predict behavior. They only suggest the pressures that are exerted in one direction or another. The middle class person will have exerted upon him the pressure of object orientation in his decisions; the mountaineer will have the pressure of person orientation. For example, the offer of a job as foreman in the mines is often refused by the person-oriented mountain man, for by becoming boss he will have to sever his ties with his fellow workers. In the coal mines, accordingly, there is almost a striving against upward advancement. The object-oriented individual will more quickly accept such a position, and will seek it eagerly, even if it means breaking the ties with fellow workmen, for he knows that he is not dependent on these ties for his individuality and that he can make other equally meaningful friendships on the new level of employment. The mountaineer would never create the kind of jealousy and strife often found in industrial plants or offices when one man is advanced over the heads of other workers who feel, for various reasons, that they should have had the promotion. Rather than destroy the harmony of the group, he would relinquish the favor.

The whole matter works conversely, however, in voluntary organizations that do not have the nature of reference groups. Feelings can be easily hurt if one person is elected over another to a place of responsibility or honor in a group such as the church or the PTA. How many mountain Sunday school superintendents are kept in office year after year because everybody knows that if they are replaced they will quit the church completely! In an object-oriented society, such elections are not taken personally and can be viewed with more calm, since the achievement of the goals of the group is at stake. The election is not seen as the acceptance or rejection of an individual person.

Such person-oriented behavior among mountain people tends to make them supersensitive to presumed slights or criticisms of their behavior: "One thing I can't stand is to be ignored or slighted." A school teacher, for example, may paddle a disobedient youngster without raising any fuss, but an insult through words or looks is taken with extreme resentment, and in older pupils may even be the cause of their dropping out of school altogether. It becomes difficult to evaluate a program after it has been held, since the security of the people taking part is so clearly bound to what went on. Any suggestion or even hint that some part of the preparation or carrying out of the program might have been done differently to advantage is likely to be taken as a personal criticism.

No person can be said to act completely as a person- or object-oriented individual. Many mountain people have been forced to act in object-oriented ways because of the great need to find a job. They move, breaking patterns of culture, in order to exist and make a living for their families. Mountain people seek a minimum of object goals, and these goals are used in return to enhance the personal relationship within the reference group. Money is a goal or object, for example, and is sought, but it is never used as a status symbol to set one person against, apart from, or above another. Never have I seen a mountaineer "lording it over" another because he has a new car or a new job or a new house. This kind of materialism is completely rejected. Mountaineers want to have their status based not on objects but on their individuality within their own group.

As person-oriented individuals, mountaineers cannot be notably successful in a business requiring any kind of personal service that is figured into the charge made to the customer. TV repairmen, for example, charge their reference-group customers (and others in the area, too, almost as if they were members of the group, as indeed some of them might someday become) with one eye on the money they need to live, but with the other eye on how the fee will suit the customer. Undercharging and overextended credit are likely to be the rule, in order to keep the customer (reference-group member) happy, and thus small businessmen find it difficult to succeed. Business is run by personal feelings rather than by good standards. One who is businesslike is suspect. "Christianity and business don't mix" is a maxim of the area. The efficient businessman is "money-mad," "a tightwad," and the "richest man in the county"— a most derisive comment. Hence he will use "business" as a reason why he cannot be involved in church or Scouts or any other "social" group. He feels that he will not be able to deal "personally" with people with whom he must also deal concerning unpaid bills or who have "beat him out of" money.

Mountaineers have a seeming disregard for the value of money, which is curiously anomalous in a money economy which places so much stress on the acquiring of material goods. There is an offhand attitude toward money, almost as if it did not matter, which is in strong contrast to the middle class striving for money as a goal in itself. Having a certain amount of money obviously does matter, since life itself depends on it, but I have seldom seen a mountaineer who seemed to care how much he was able to get or to save. Other things are much more important to him.

A similar disregard for time is also part of the mountain man's make-up. He lives by rhythms other than the hour, day or week. The rhythms of the shifts at the mine, of hunting and fishing seasons, of gardening—these provide the paces for his life. The particular hour of the day is of less concern to him than it is to the middle class person.

His person orientation makes him much more aware of his person-to-person relationships than of a time schedule which must be kept. He cares far more about keeping a friendly relationship with a neighbor whom he has met on the way to a meeting than about being there on time. This is one very important point that middle class persons must be aware of as they have dealings with mountain people. In the middle class world, a man can impersonally do what business needs to be done with a person, then proceed elsewhere. In the folk culture, you don't just stop in for a moment to check on a detail or two of business, then move on. Each contact is a person-to-person encounter, and this takes time—hours of it. A trip to the store, going to the neighbors' to borrow a cup of sugar or an ax, meeting a friend on the road—these are not impersonal encounters, in which the business at hand can be done quickly, but are occasions for the kinds of personal relationships that form the very core of the mountain man's existence.

A county school official recently discussed his efforts to see three men who were being chosen for a special training program. It took him six hours, because—as he noted— "you can't do business with these people on a time schedule." You must also "set a spell," and in the midst of this person-to-person meeting any business you may have can be done. The impersonal manner of business dealing common to the middle class simply will not do for the mountaineer.

Because the mountaineer personalizes, he finds it difficult to understand the bureaucracies of business and government. He has a certain fear of them, as if those who run them were out to get him or were interested only in doing things to their own advantage and at his expense. Thus government is evil, and anyone who goes into politics becomes corrupted. "Never elect a good man to office; it will ruin him" is an expression that is often heard. If a particular office of the government does not serve the mountaineer's own personal needs, it is therefore corrupt or not doing its proper job. Some of the local party representatives conceive of victory only as a means of pressuring the government to get favors for their district and people. By personalizing impersonal relationships, the mountain man sees all forms of government as dishonest and scheming against him. He regards himself as being exploited by government and by business—and, indeed, this has happened often enough to justify his feelings.

Because the orientation of the mountaineer's life is toward his family and peers, he conceives of all his moral principles in relation to this reference group. Such principles as honesty, fairness, equality, justice, reciprocity, charity, and one I shall call "person-ality" (in contrast to impersonality), he relates to the group. In dealing outside the group, he expects the same relationship to exist. Such an expectation is obviously unrealistic. The government official cannot deal with the mountaineer's individual problem as if he were a member of the mountaineer's reference group; the doctor cannot devote himself to him in sickness as a reference group member would; the businessman cannot treat all his customers as if they were members of the family; nor can the minister give the kind of care and attention that family members are expected to give. Thus the mountaineer often views these relationships with bitterness and suspicion. So he maintains his person-oriented stance and wants the world to adopt it, too.

Since the outside world does not conform to this pattern, the mountaineer feels that he can reject it as basically evil and, as he rejects it, finds himself rejecting as well education, the structure of life necessary for business and commerce, the profit motive, art and drama, organized amusements, style in clothing, and almost anything modern. This rejection can be viewed as sour grapes, since the mountaineer's poverty makes it impossible for him to attain these things whatever his outlook might be. But the mountaineer's attitude should not be rationalized so simply. There is a style of life in the mountains that finds these things foreign, and thus unattractive. It has been interesting, however, to watch the inroads that TV, for example, has made in mountain homes. For a time, it was strictly forbidden as evil, but it has gradually gained acceptance, until now almost every home has in its central room the very symbol of the outside world, drumming its wares into every ear and flashing them before every eye. One of my coworkers says, with some truth, that TV has done more to change the ideas of mountain people in ten years than the church has done in generations.

4.

The Mountaineer in His Society

THE social life as well as the emotional security of the
mountain person is centered in the reference group, within which all important activities take place. This central
group, which is composed of persons of the same sex and
status and of approximately the same age, shapes the mountaineer's personality and his culture. He finds his fulfillment
as a person within this primary group. There are no strict
rules for defining this group, but for adults it is almost entirely family based, including the immediate family, cousins,
and uncles, with a few close neighbors. Compatibility is
essential, so that not all members of a family are in a given
reference group, only those who get along well together.
This group is dominant throughout the mountaineer's life;
its composition changes only slowly, as persons within it die
or move away or as new ones are added. So strong is the
reference-group structure of the society that even husbands
and wives tend to pull away from each other toward their
respective reference groups. Spouses do not share the same
group, since a group is not heterosexually composed. In contrast, reference groups in middle class American culture are
much less prominent in the structure of life, and the husband
and wife tend to pull away from the group toward each
other, having activities and social life in common.

The mountains contain great numbers of these reference
groups. There is communication between them by means
of persons who are members of more than one group. These

persons convey information from one group to another, providing a very effective means of passing news along. Thus does one group keep tabs on all the others. These groups have a tremendous hold over their members, through subtle (and sometimes not so subtle) pressures making them conform to the unspoken, unwritten "code" and binding them to the mountain culture with great tenacity.

Let everyone who works in the Appalachian South take cognizance of the power of these reference groups, which stand at the very center of the mountaineer's life. To step out of the group would mean loss of identity. To stand out in the group or to try to change the group from within is practically impossible, for one would quickly be ostracized. Any outsider who tries to change the reference group is very likely to find himself rejected by it.

THE FAMILY

The mountain family is a closely knit one, not because of shared activities but because of emotional dependence. In fact, the casual observer looking in on a household could easily catch the feeling that here are persons who live side by side in the same house but have little else to do with each other. Few recreations are ever shared. Christmas is about the only holiday that is looked forward to or for which special plans are made. One of our staff members has made a practice of seeing that every person who comes to the church has a small gift on his birthday, as a means of showing that each person is special. This is a novelty and is received eagerly by young and old alike.

While the social ties of the family are often not strong, being related as they are to the reference groups, the emotional and dependency ties are extremely strong. The death of a family member brings great and, what seems to the casual observer, even exaggerated grief. I have seen adults who for years have shown little concern for their parents break completely at the word that their father or mother is seriously ill or has died. Graveyards (which are often family plots) are kept cleaned off and almost always covered with flowers in remembrance of a loved one. I have seen parents who seemed unconcerned about their children's training refuse to let the child be away from home for even a night. This nuclear family is quite open-ended, accepting into its midst with apparent ease a daughter whose husband has left her, or an unwanted child (illegitimate or otherwise) of a daughter or a close relative, or an aged aunt or cousin. Both sons and daughters want to settle near their parents, and whole hollows or bottoms have gradually filled up with the houses of kin settling close to each other.

The mountaineer's home is generally not a large one, especially considering his extra-large family. Sometimes every room but the kitchen is filled with beds. One bedroom serves as a kind of sitting room, in one corner of which is the TV set. Thus home cannot be a gathering place for the youth, as it is in a society where one room is free for socializing. The house itself tends to emphasize the adult-centeredness of the family.

Meals are not usually a family affair but are taken cafeteria style. The mother prepares the supper, and when the first bus arrives from school those children eat; when the second bus arrives, the second shift begins; when the father comes in from work, he eats, and finally the mother herself eats alone or with the smaller children, who probably have already eaten what they wanted with the others.

I am always amazed at the lack of planning in the social life of mountain folk. Visiting is almost always done on the whim of the moment. If it is mealtime, a visitor is urged to "stay and see how poor folks live," but planning ahead to invite friends to dinner is rare. The family reunion is the one big, planned social effort, sometimes attended by several hundred persons. It is held outdoors in the summer on the "home church" grounds or in a specially prepared grove. Sometimes tables and benches and a small shelter for the speakers' stand are kept for this once-a-year occasion when all the scattered members of the family gather. Local members of the family bring table service and baskets of food and spread the sumptuous feast for all to share. As usual, the men gather together, the young people form their groups, small children care for littler ones, and the women bustle about. After dinner, specially invited groups of singers perform, and there is usually preaching, by more than one person, or addresses by political figures.

Church suppers, the potluck affairs that are so common and so enjoyed in some places, are usually not well attended. Often the persons who do come have already eaten at home, and show up just for the fellowship and a cup of coffee. As the individuals who do eat finish, they get up immediately and go apart to talk, rather than sitting around the tables to converse for a time, as in middle class society.

CHILDREN AND THE FAMILY

Babies have a unique place in the mountain family. Though the mountain man often pays little attention to the larger children, he will make a great deal of fuss over babies, playing with them, fondling them, and carrying them about. Even older boys are this way. I have seen teen-age boys take a crying infant from its mother's arms during church, amusing it for the rest of the service with an interest and tenderness which is almost unbelievable in the light of the usual male role.

Each child is welcomed happily into the family, no matter how many there already are or how poor the family is. Large families are considered a blessing; for many years past, the more children there were, the more help there was in making a living. Eight or more children are not at all uncommon. Until very recently, death rates were very high among children, and there is hardly an older family that does not keep a small hillside grave plot where sons and daughters are buried. In the past few years, families have become smaller, yet the highest birth rates in the nation are still in the mountains (Leslie County, Kentucky, has the highest). Methods of family planning are generally unknown, although we have not found great opposition to them. For generations, circumstances have fostered a "live for today" philosophy. The difficulty and uncertainty of life have led most mountain people to accept whatever comes along, including children. Children are highly valued because they give meaning to the parents' lives. One mother expressed it, "If I didn't have my children, I wouldn't have nothin'." Another, speaking of her nine-year-old son, her only child, said, "Yes, I dress him and tie his shoes. It's my pleasure to do it as long as he's at home." I am confident that one reason for the high rate of illegitimate births in the mountains is that the arrival of a child gives a young girl a new sense of her own purpose and worth: her child needs her. I know of few cases where such children are given up for adoption. Many times a married daughter will give a newborn child to her mother to keep; the mother did not have any little ones to care for, while the daughter already had several. Many mountain children are brought up by grandparents. These tangled relationships are so common that school nurses have learned to say, "What name do you go by?" instead of "What is your name?" in filling out immunization cards. In the space marked "Father's name" they quickly accept the response, "My mother's name is——"

The fact that babies are not planned affects not only the way in which parents relate to them but also the methods by which they are reared. American society today is characterized by three types of families: the *adult-centered*—prevalent in the mountain and working class groups, run by adults, where the children are expected to behave as much like adults as possible; the *child-centered*—found among middle class families, in which children are planned for and in which the parents subordinate their wishes and pleasures to give the child what they think he needs; and the *adult-directed*—an upper middle class pattern, in which parents also place lower priorities on their own needs, in order to guide their children toward the goals planned.[1]

In the middle classes, where children are planned for and the husband and wife share a great deal in their common life, the presence of the children reinforces the relationship between husband and wife. Parents find themselves communicating with each other through the rearing of their children. Parents sacrifice for their children, play with them, carry on many activities with them. Much of the parental concern is to provide for the children—good environment, good schools, wholesome recreation. Participating in Scouts, church, or Little League with the children helps achieve these goals. When children are appearing in special programs at school or church or club, parents make an effort to be present. Their goals for the children may include a college education, or having a happier childhood than they themselves had, or a happier home, or more comforts. These families may be said to be child-centered.

In the professional or upper middle class, the parents are usually college-educated and have arrived at a station in life in which they feel secure. Because the wife is often

[1] Herbert J. Gans, *The Urban Villagers* (New York: Free Press of Glencoe, 1962), pp. 54 ff.

educated, her interests may well extend beyond the home. These parents know more plainly what they want for their children than does the child-centered family. Their relationship may be said to be adult-directed. The child's desires are less important than his goals. Much time and effort will be spent to assure the child's success in school in order that he may be a proper adult, achieving his goals. His parents will exert considerable pressure on him to excel in whatever he undertakes.

The mountain family is adult-centered. Since children are not planned, their arrival does not put them at the family center. They are born into a family that for generations has built its life around making a living from the hard environment of the steep hillsides and the narrow valleys. Making a living (for the male) and making a home (for the female) have been the consuming pursuits of mountain life. Children are expected to fit into this life pattern as soon as they are able.

THE TRAINING OF CHILDREN

While the child is still a baby and does not object to being an adult's toy, he is part of the world of his parents. As he begins to have a mind of his own and to challenge the authority of his parents, adult ego satisfaction diminishes and the process of separation begins. As children grow, they are more and more allowed to form their own reference groups, and parents cease to play with them as soon as they mature beyond infancy. There is a curiously unchildlike quality about mountain children; one sees and hears little spontaneous laughter and enthusiasm and few group games. Children are not allowed play that interferes with adult life. Girls are expected to become little mothers, and boys are given a great deal of freedom, just as their fathers are. When someone calls on the family, the children will either be shooed off to another room while the grown-ups talk or else required to sit quietly. Seldom are the children present introduced as part of the family or allowed to participate in the conversation; almost never are they brought from other parts of the house to be introduced, and they are most certainly not allowed to dominate the scene even for a moment.

At community gatherings or family reunions, parents will abandon the younger children to the care of their older sisters while the adults talk or participate in the program. They will notice the children only when discipline is clearly called for. And children gravitate to their reference groups quickly in any gathering. The family pew is unheard of in the mountains. Girls and young boys may sit with their mothers, older boys never. Their group gathers outside or sits together in the back. Church is an adult activity, and adults actually seem oblivious to the misbehavior of their children on the back rows. Parents reprimand their children for misbehavior but seldom offer specific, positive teaching.

Mountain children are reared impulsively, with relatively little of the conscious training found in middle class families. Discipline is meted out with no concern about how the child will react as a child. In such an adult-centered society, children's feelings are not given great weight. When they misbehave, they are punished—and it is always physical punishment, not just a scolding or being sent to their rooms. The ubiquitous apple tree switch is always handy, and its use is quickly threatened for the least offense. Many a slight mountain mother can still use that switch with effect on a teenage son who may be larger than she, and he figures that she has the right to do it. In situations calling for ordinary punishment, she administers the switch herself. If the misdeed is thought to be bad enough, she will wait for her husband to come home. Then, however, if she feels he is punishing too severely, she will intercede for her child. There are times when she may even enter into a conspiracy with the child to prevent the father from finding out about something that would surely bring down his wrath. Punishment is not given in order to press toward a desired result, it is simply to keep the child in line. Because the father tends to be unreasonable in his administering of punishment, and the mother can often be counted on to be overly lenient or can be talked into leniency, the child's strong emotional attachment to "Mommy" is encouraged.

This training, based as it is on the fear of punishment, builds into the child either a resentment toward or a fear of authority of any kind. Rewards are given or promised if children behave or do something which the parents desire them to do. "If you pass your grade, I'll give you a dollar"; likewise, "If you fail your grade, you'll get a whipping."

Child rearing in mountain families is not only impulsive but permissive and indulgent as well. Children are seldom required to do what they do not want to do. I have even known of sick children who, on finding their medicine distasteful, were allowed not to take it, even though their welfare depended upon their doing so. If a child wants candy or pop he can have it, even though his teeth may be rotting out because of it. If a child does not particularly want to have a new experience (going to camp, for example), parents seldom urge him to go for the good it might do him. They let the child make the decision. Kephart, many years ago, noted this aspect of child rearing: "Most mountaineers are indulgent, super-indulgent parents. . . . The boys, especially, grow up with little restraint beyond their own natural sense of filial duty. Little children are allowed to eat or drink anything they want. . . ."[2] There is little in the moun-

---

[2] Horace Kephart, *Our Southern Highlanders* (New York: Outing Publishing Co., 1913), p. 82.

tain child's training that would help him develop self-control, discipline, resolution, or steadfastness. Thus the way is prepared for future difficulties in the army or at work. In his adult life he tends to be capricious, vacillating, and volatile. His feelings are easily hurt; he will quit groups when things don't go his way, and otherwise demonstrate immature behavior.

Mothers tell their children what they expect of them, yet often do not insist on the command's being carried out. I have seen mothers keep up a constant stream of commands and suggestions which the children ignored completely, appearing not even to hear. The command of the father, however, is more likely to be heeded. Children soon learn that words do not count as much as action. They learn that their mother's torrents of words do not mean as much as the impulsive paddling they receive on occasion. They quickly catch on to the technique of appearing to obey for a moment, in order to go right back to whatever they were about without fear of further interference for a time. Because of this training, young people are not taught to listen to what words mean, but only to what emotion the speaker is conveying. Hence it is extremely difficult for teachers, social workers, ministers, and others to communicate with mountain people. The workers believe that the words themselves, their meaning and arrangement, convey the message. Mountain people "hear" the feeling behind the words. This type of child rearing is basically a conservative one, as one might imagine, being limited by what is already done rather than being pointed toward a goal that might be attained or an ideal that could be reached.

While middle class families tend to have a clear image of the future educational achievement, social status, or kind of life they hope their children will have, and so work toward that end, the mountaineer has no such aims in view. Often the mountaineer's goals for his children are couched in negative terms—what he does not want them to be. Coal miners usually do not want their sons to mine coal, nor do small farmers want their sons to follow in their footsteps. All that mountain people know is that they do want their children to "make good," to get enough education (although they are not sure how much is necessary) and to have a more secure life than they have had. Few know how to go about achieving these goals. If children go wrong, parents often blame the reference group and do not assume the same responsibility or sense of guilt that middle class families would.

MOUNTAIN YOUTH

As children grow, the gulf between them and their parents increases. Adult reference groups have little relationship to either child or youth reference groups. Adult society, accordingly, has little constructive influence in young lives. The adults seem utterly baffled by the young people, not knowing what to do to help them and being almost afraid to try anything. It becomes very difficult; therefore, to find adults who have much interest or success in leading either church or community youth groups. The training of mountain youth consists largely of imitation of their peers as they in turn imitate adults.

These youth reference groups largely operate outside the home, which tends to be small and crowded and adult-dominated. Unlike his city counterpart, the mountain youth still has some home chores. He brings in coal or water and cuts kindling wood. In the more rural areas, youths are kept fairly close to home to help in the garden or with the animals. Once finished with the required chores, the boys, especially, are free to join their friends. It is common to see groups of them gathered on the porch of a country store or under a large tree where the river forks, or perched on a culvert railing. In these groups the boys find their social outlet. I have known boys who were sullen and uncommunicative at home to become talkative and ebullient when they were with a group of particular friends. The boys plan and carry out contests of strength and physical prowess, teach one another about sex (few mountain parents will talk about it to their children), and generally exert a very conservative influence on each other. For example, any boy in the group who does well in school, or who studies hard, or who sets goals for his life which he tells the group about, becomes the object of ridicule; he either succumbs to the pressure or else is dropped from the group altogether. By this means is group solidarity maintained. It is nothing short of tragedy that these reference groups can exert such pressure on the individual boy without being countered by any adult influence. The youth's life is so involved with these groups, his security so bound up with them, that few are strong enough to go their own way outside them. Adults do not know and seem hardly to care what goes on in these groups, so long as there is no community trouble resulting from the boys' activities. Adolescent society, in short, is very much unguided by experienced adults. Boys teach boys and girls teach girls. It is no wonder that mountain culture tends to perpetuate itself in traditional ways.

The girls are far less likely to belong to such separate reference groups than are the boys. Girls have far less freedom, partly because they have more home chores and partly because families feel more protective toward them. Girls are often found in groups of two or three and are more likely to be in someone's home. Boys are expected to "protect" their sisters. There is a close feeling between the brothers and sisters in the families, and the boys are taught that they have a responsibility to look after their sisters. Fairly small boys will walk quite a distance to escort a sister to a neighbor's house, then walk back again to escort her home.

Dating begins about the junior-high age. The nature of mountain society invites troubles immediately: there is nothing to do. For teenagers, life is incredibly dull. They are filled with vague restlessness and longings, and there are neither intellectual nor recreational outlets for them. Little money is available to them, further cutting down their ability to do things. Allowances on a regular basis, either for work done or simply because a certain amount is needed regularly for school, are not at all common. When a young person needs money, he asks his father (usually) for it each time—even if he needs it every day, as for school lunches. This is another aspect of the person-centeredness of the society. Getting or not getting the money is dependent upon the whim of the father at the time. Thus young people soon learn how to "soap up the old man" in order to get what they want. It may be they enlist their mother in the process of getting money out of the father. Few arrangements are made in the family on the basis of impersonal justice or need. What is done is dependent upon the feeling of the giver at the moment of asking, or upon the persuasive skill of the requester.

"What do you do on a date?" I have asked young people. "There ain't nothin' to do. You can go over to her house and watch television if they have one, but chances are her folks are sittin' right there with you and hardly even talk to you." And there is no other place to go. A boy and girl dating seldom join with other couples. In all kinds of weather you see young couples out walking along the roads. They have no adult guidance and nothing to do. Is it any wonder that the illegitimate birth rate of the mountain area has always been high?

Illegitimacy is common and is more accepted than it is

in middle class society. Adult society seems to say, "We had nothing to do with the situation, and we can't do anything about it. Might just as well accept it." Sometimes the boy is required to marry the girl; often he is not. The girl will keep her baby; she may quit school to tend it, or perhaps she will give it to her mother to keep and bring up. Because babies are so highly regarded in mountain families, illegitimate children are welcomed gladly and spoiled with the rest. The baby's mother quickly takes her place in society again, sometimes even in her old reference group, as if nothing had happened. Even though she has had one or more children, a girl is still very eligible for marriage. Either the grandparents will add the illegitimate children to their family or the husband will accept them as if they were his own. Putting these children up for adoption is not only practically unheard of in the mountains, it is thought to be a cruel practice. How could the unwed mother, or the grandparents, even think of giving up their own child to a stranger!

There is actually very little delinquency in the mountains. The gangs of boys will get into various kinds of devilment just for amusement; a group in one valley may have fights with groups from adjacent valleys or develop intense rivalries with them. Mailboxes may be removed, windows in old buildings broken out, apples stolen, outhouses dismantled and moved, or chickens stolen for a feast. Occasionally tires and gas will be stolen from cars to provide for a vehicle that the boys will use. But few premeditated, vicious acts are ever done. Senseless mugging, or destruction of school property, or molesting of older people is almost unheard of. This is partly because the rural nature of the area provides plenty of room to work off pent-up emotions. A good hike in the mountains, exploring caves or rolling boulders down a hill just to hear them crash, going hunting or fishing—this kind of activity is readily available and provides physical and emotional outlets for the boys. A second reason for the low rate of delinquency is the person-centeredness of the society. When we asked some of the boys why they don't act in the delinquent ways that some city youths do, they replied, "Why, these are our own people, our friends and neighbors. We couldn't do things like that to them!" It wouldn't be easy to get away with it unrecognized, either.

In any society, young people often utter remarks like "I hate school" or "I wish school would get out sooner." In other cultures, these feelings, which are fairly common, are not allowed to gain much influence. Parents quickly squelch such statements, and the overall pressure of society is directed toward making good in school. But among the reference groups of mountain youth, where adult influence is almost nonexistent, this feeling is allowed to grow and predominate. Many young people either put forth just enough effort in school to be kept on the ball team, or drop out early and thereby gain status in the reference group.

Church activities are regarded in the same way. As long as the church can provide some excitement for their dull lives, young people will be found at church. Few can make any serious commitment to the church, because the pressure of the reference group is against it—unless, as occasionally happens, a whole group can be enlisted together.

MARRIAGE

While childhood seems to be only a waiting period until adulthood is attained, adolescence is in many ways the high point of life—especially the courting period, and especially for girls. At this time, for once in their lives, girls have a significance and honor and have some attention paid to them. It is a brief moment, remembered with nostalgia, for marriage comes early for many. Family life for the adolescent is often very unhappy. Marriage presents the promise, at least, of some escape. Parents have no insight into youthful feelings and do not try to understand. Since neither educational nor vocational plans stand in the way, parents feel they can do no other than let young people marry when they wish. Many marry in order to get away from home, succeeding only in setting up another household where the same problems are perpetuated. Even in this rebellious breaking away, the youths are still tied emotionally to their parents, hating them yet needing them. The bridal glow very soon disappears, and the slow, dull pace of life sets in with added responsibilities and frustrations. After marriage, mountain women seem to age quickly, becoming passive and less conscious of themselves as being attractive than are middle class women. The men, while going through a somewhat similar pattern, are freer in their choices and activities, and do not seem to age so quickly.

Though mountain young people are romantic to a degree, the wedding is often thought of as "doing what's necessary" rather than being an experience that is planned for, savored, and remembered. Often the young couple will just "decide to get married" one weekend, going to the courthouse for the tests and license and then going to find any "preacher" who will perform the service right away—with neither parents nor friends sharing the experiences. No honeymoon is planned, and the bride and groom may return to one of their families immediately after the service to begin living together while they plan where and how they will live permanently. Sometimes they live for some weeks or months with either parent, apparently experiencing little conflict with them. Often the boy has no job.

Very soon after the marriage, the romantic side disappears and each spouse takes up again with the reference-group friends of the same sex. Family life patterns are largely molded by this pull and the resulting lack of communication, as husband and wife lead almost separate existences side by side. Elizabeth Bott describes this relationship between husband and wife as "segregated," in contrast to the "joint" relationship of the middle class couple, and notes that it results in a separation of tasks, friends, leisure-time pursuits, interests, and activities.[3] The fact of marriage, moreover, does not mean that the basic emotional dependence of the couple is changed. Dependence on "Mommy" and "Daddy" is preserved intact. Thus, if either spouse needs to be hospitalized, and a decision must be made by the family in consultation with the doctors, the other spouse is not the one consulted; it is the parents of the sick one that are called in to decide.

Once my wife and I invited a group of young couples to a New Year's Eve party; children were left at home. Several couples remarked that it was the first time in many years (for one couple it was twelve years) that they had done anything together as husbands and wives. In counseling couples who are having marital troubles, I have often found that they have nothing in common. He resents her wasting time gossiping with her friends all day long, and she resents his going off every evening to play cards or talk with his friends, leaving her alone. Middle class persons often find it difficult to accept what seems to them a total unconcern of husband and wife for each other; yet this pattern has been common for people of the mountains for generations. The husband was often taken by death in the mines or through the hardness and hazards of frontier life, and the wife would be forced to carry on by herself to keep the family together. Likewise, illness or death in childbirth might remove the woman before her time. This lack of closeness has made it easier for the remaining parent to maintain the household,

[3] *Family and Social Network* (London: Tavistock Publications, 1957), pp. 53-54.

along with the help of the extended family. It is remarkable how many such broken-by-death families exist in the mountains.

The fact that a reference group is either all men or all women means that there is a distinct separation of the male and female roles. The males are less adept in a heterosexual relationship than are the females. When people get together, the men gather in one group, the women in another. Only during the adolescent courting period is this pattern broken to any extent or for any length of time. Sunday school classes are often divided in this way, and it is even common in church worship services to have the men sitting on one side or in one section and the women and children in another. Though this pattern of separation of the sexes is common in many societies, in mountain society it is extreme.

In middle class society the tasks connected with the home are also partly the man's duty. He expects to clean the garage or the basement or to relieve his wife of the care of the children for a time, will help with the dishes or laundry, and may even enjoy cooking. In mountain culture, however, the lines of duty are drawn much more rigidly, and seldom are the tasks assigned to one spouse shared by the other. When the husband comes home from work, no wife asks him to help in the house or with the children. Many a coal miner, on getting home from work, finds his wife almost his obedient slave, having the water hot for his bath (sometimes heated in pans on top of a stove in the wash house out back), with clean clothes all laid out and supper ready. Few wives would dare to be absent when their husbands come home. The husband's task is to earn the living. The wife's duty is to care for the house and family; often she even tends the garden or the yard and does the inside painting. Gardening, however, is acceptable male work.

The sexes tend to be uncomfortable with each other, and

few words pass between them. The man's inability to converse with women is part of a traditional pattern. In the hard life of the frontier the father and boys had to work outdoors; few social contacts were made or were necessary, and few social skills were developed. The pursuits of farming, logging, and mining, or of hunting and fishing, actually prevent the learning of social skills. Often, too, the mountain male has less education than the female, and he will not place himself in a position where a "smarter" woman can show him up. He functions best when he is with his own reference group.

Girls, on the other hand, are brought up in a more social environment. While learning sewing and cooking and housekeeping, they also learn social skills as a byproduct. In a society which has exalted male dominance in the form of authority and strength, these have been her defense. The mountain male often retreats to cover in the face of a "good talkin'" woman, wholly inadequate to compete. This, in a sense, has been the mountain woman's main weapon against her husband. She may not be able to command; but she can talk her way to what she wants.

The mountaineer is always wary of heterosexual encounters and deliberately shuns them. In making home visits for the church on a financial or evangelistic canvass, for example, men go with men and women with women. Pastors indigenous to the area often take either their wives or some male member calling with them, since it would not be considered proper for a man to go visiting where a woman might be present alone.

THE CHANGING ROLE OF THE SEXES

Gradually, under the force of economic circumstance, the male role has been changing. The mountain man who is no longer able to be the breadwinner, no longer able to make his own independent way, has lost his traditional reason for living. No one wants his strength. In the mines, machines have replaced the pick and shovel and the strong arm. Frustrated at every turn, the mountaineer has suffered a loss of self, of worth. Once the dominant member of the family, he is now its burden. Forced to sit at home, unemployed, while his family suffers or becomes the object of various forms of relief, he becomes discouraged and beaten. Because this has happened not just to individual men but to the entire society, the whole image of maleness has suffered.

The mountain man has found, on moving to the cities, that his better-educated wife can more easily get and keep a job, while he must stay at home to keep the house and children. Even if he stays in the mountains, his wife is more likely to find a job than he—doing housework, keeping a store, or serving in a nearby clinic or hospital. He has come to see that the education he never got (or wanted) is the very thing that the society holds up to him as necessary. One by one the symbols of his maleness have fallen.

The mountain woman, however, has not been subjected to this kind of humiliating need for changes in her role. Her place in the family as wife and mother has remained intact. If the family has had to move, her ability to socialize has stood her in good stead in the outside world. Thus, bit by bit, as her husband's role has decreased and as his life has lost its meaning, her life has taken on new meaning in the community or at work. This situation is leading to a reversal of the roles of the sexes in mountain life. The woman is becoming the strong one, able to make decisions and cope with the increasingly complex world that is reaching in. A matriarchal society is developing; as it does, the male becomes all the more baffled in his existence and a burden to his family— with tremendous effects on family, church, and community life.

Before some of the present government aid programs went

into effect, the epitome of irony was found in the situation where the family could get no relief as long as an employable male was at home. In order to enable his wife and children to be provided for, even in a minimal way, the husband had to abandon them. Then his wife could apply for relief assistance for the family. The father might still live close by, but he always had to be careful not to be found by the welfare worker. Thus, in order to have his family provided for, he was forced to make himself invisible. Few schemes more destructive of the mountaineer's sense of his own worth could have been devised. It is devastating enough for the middle class man to lose his job and place as breadwinner for his family; such a loss of position destroys the mountain man's inmost self.

ADULT REFERENCE GROUP LIFE

In working class or folk society, as has been noted, social life revolves around the reference group. This is not to say that this social life is comparable to the middle class round of parties, friends to dinner, or evenings out. Rather, it takes the form of more casual, almost daily encounters to exchange gossip and news and to compare ideas. The more limited the outlook of the persons involved, the more likely is the reference group to be confined to family members, and the less comfortable the person will be in outside contacts. The more upwardly mobile persons, those exhibiting more nearly middle class tendencies, will belong to one or more groups composed of like-minded friends, who will most often be close neighbors. The women are often found talking over the back fence or having coffee in the kitchen. The men can be found on the porch, or on the steps of a nearby store, chatting away about the latest rumors regarding work, or relishing stories of the mines or mountains which they tell with great skill.

Herbert Gans describes the reference-group society as being held together by rubber, alternately stretching and contracting as the various members of the group vie and jockey with each other for recognition or acceptance.[4] It is within this group that one is able to express one's individuality. Though some are looked to as natural leaders and do more of the talking, practically everybody in the group is able to relate what he knows, tell a story, or give an opinion. Considerable joking and teasing go on as the members test each other out. Outside the group, mountain people are often uncommunicative, almost sullen, but within it they take on new life and expression. If a man's "turn" is unusually quiet, even in the group, he is accepted in this role. It may thus be said that one's personality is whole only in interaction with this particular group of persons.

Subjects that might engender conflict are not discussed. For people so dependent on relationships, any kind of slight or hurt is devastating to both happiness and security. And since new ideas are hard for the mountaineer to handle, persons who differ with him are at least suspect and may become enemies. A give-and-take discussion where differing opinions, honestly held, are expressed is not common to reference-group conversations. When splits do occur, they are deep and lasting, and the techniques for healing them are unknown. In counseling couples before marriage, I have often tried to find out how the bride and groom express their anger, in an effort to point to ways of settling differences within their marriage relationship. Time and again comes the statement, "I never get angry with anybody in the family," which means "We all agree to stay away from controversial subjects" or "I bottle it up inside myself."

The closeness of this interrelated reference group means that there are always strong tensions which are not at all

[4] Gans, p. 81.

visible to the outsider. They are generally kept under control, for everyone in the group knows how far he can safely go. But when someone does go too far, the blowup appears much too large to the outsider, because he cannot feel the tremendous undercurrent which has been present all along. Such blowups affect large segments of the community; clubs, PTA, churches and other ongoing activities inherit reference-group troubles.

Relations in the reference group are equalitarian, and there seems to be an almost total disregard for the kind of status represented by the "keeping up with the Joneses" attitude. The fickleness of the economic situation through the years has reduced the possibility of this kind of behavior to a minimum. No family could depend from day to day on having any material security, and so status based on possessions was never structured into the culture. There is a great deal of extravagant impulse buying of furniture and appliances, but seldom, if ever, are such acquisitions used for rising above the neighbors or the reference group. New cars are a status symbol only to the young boys, who are quickly disabused of such thoughts after marriage or a few years of poverty living. The stratification that does exist seems to be based on external morality. People "look down on" drunks, adulterers, and people who don't pay debts, and the more stable look down on those who can't keep a job or don't keep clean.

Since one of the main functions of the reference group is to provide a means of individual expression, the members are not really interested in the achievement of goals or in joint activities. The group is unable to function to achieve desired goals unless all share them. If group tasks are presented, there is always the fear that dissension will occur over decisions that need to be made or that the group will be manipulated or used by the leaders to gain power over the rest. Hence it is always difficult to find those within the society who will dare to risk the danger of separation from the group in order to undertake leadership responsibilities or even to take a stand on any issue. A classic example of this reluctance to make a stand on anything for fear of cutting oneself off from the group or causing hard feeling was an incident in which a new postmaster wished to move the post office to a building closer to his home. He began circulating a petition among the citizens to support his request to the Post Office Department. Another man in the community, at that point, began also to circulate a petition opposing the move, since he wished the post office to remain close to *his* home. When the petitions were in, it was found that almost all of the citizens involved had signed both petitions.

Outside of the reference group, the mountaineer is uneasy, even suspicious. When he is sufficiently motivated to go beyond the group—to the PTA for instance—he is often unwilling to enter into any discussion and refuses to vote when a possibly controversial issue must be decided. There are usually upwardly mobile people present who will do the talking and say what they think. Then, naturally, they are accused of "running things." The fear of criticism (which may never be uttered but often imagined) is the weapon the reference group holds over its members. Thus it acts as a conservative force, molding its members quite effectively and keeping the society in a state of near stagnation. It would take a strong person, indeed, to go counter to the reference group, for he would not only be ostracized from his social life but would lose his source of security and individuality as well. County judges recognize this fact and sometimes sentence habitual troublemakers to complete separation from their reference groups by banning them from the county where they get into trouble.

LEAVING THE FAMILY

Loyalty to the family and the reference group is built into the cultural structure of the mountains. Persons who leave the family find life very difficult. In fact, the middle class axiom that the task of the parent is to bring up his child so that the child won't need him any more but can be independent is simply not at all true of mountain culture. Almost the opposite is true. No mountain parent would dream of bringing up a child in such a way. A child is brought up to become part of the family and reference group.

Families that migrate to the city often move into the same neighborhood (or even the same house) as other mountain families, to the consternation of landlords. City officials and ordinary citizens frown on the formation of such new ghettos; yet this is part of the pattern one would expect. When uprooted, these families seek to recreate their mountain culture as nearly as possible.

The mountaineer does not join in with the neighborhood groups or the larger organizations of the city, which are often operated on very impersonal bases. Partly through fear of impersonal social contacts, and partly from the traditional pull of the family group to center in itself, he does not enter fully into city life. This reluctance increases his alienation. When middle class persons move from one city to another, as often happens in our mobile culture, they find substitutes for their friends and peers. "People are much the same wherever you go" is a common phrase. But mountain families do not often say this when they are forced to move, because no one can replace the family in the security pattern. Nor does distance in miles break the psychological dependency ties. Many mountain families who have been living in the city for years would move back to the mountains in a minute if they could be assured of jobs there. The fierce loyalty of mountain people to home is mostly a loyalty to the only culture in which they feel secure and which operates in ways they know and appreciate. This is one reason, at least, why armchair economists who say that the only answer to the Southern Appalachian unemployment problem is migration, answer too simply. From the vantage point of middle or upper class culture, moving is easy. For the mountaineer, moving is a kind of death to his way of life. It cuts him off from his sustaining roots.

THE REFERENCE GROUP AND THE SELF

Since every part of the mountain man's life is aimed toward person-to-person encounter, he finds it difficult to react to situations in other than personal ways. He relates almost every new possibility or every new plan to himself. This attitude could well lead an outsider to believe that the mountaineer is a very selfish person. Actually, to those within his reference group he is more than generous, and he is even so to others in the area. I know one man who is working, for example, to assist as many as five other families whose breadwinners are out of work; he gives them food and money for utilities. And yet, his individualism does make the mountaineer "look out for himself."

Because the mountain man finds his self-identification mainly in his relationship with others, he has never developed a satisfactory self-image as a single individual. He is only somebody in relation to his peers. Thus he finds it difficult to accept a particular "role" either in his family or in another group—as teacher of others or leader of a meeting. He tries, but he always slips back into the personal, nonreflective role of reference-group participant. In contrast, the middle class person can present to a group a particular cause or position that perhaps does not even involve him personally. He may even present a position he does not share, in order to have both sides heard. When he becomes chairman, he can separate himself from the group, and because he has object goals toward which he seeks to guide the group, he can function as an effective leader. The mountaineer, because he has no image of himself as a person, can involve himself only impulsively, directly, and personally in such situations. He can enter in only without reflection. Because object goals are not primary in his life, as a leader he may be very ineffective; the meetings he leads are directed more toward satisfactory interpersonal relationships and feeling than toward any goal which the group might have. This fact makes the task of finding and training leaders for groups within the mountains extremely difficult. In short, when the mountaineer can act impulsively within the security of the reference group, he feels at home. Outside this group, when he must act in thought-out ways he feels himself at a disadvantage. He is unsure of himself, tends to depreciate himself and his abilities, will lapse into shyness or even fear. This combination of forces makes it very difficult to get volunteers to take on particular jobs. Within the reference group, to volunteer would mean to step out unduly from the rest, while outside the reference group to volunteer would be to make a frightening move into the unknown.

This inability to relate to persons on other than a personal basis, which the impulsive child-rearing practices of the mountain family no doubt help to foster, also tends to make the mountaineer suspicious of the outsider. "If you want to be friendly, that is one thing, but if you want to do something for me or to me, that is another," is almost the attitude. Indeed, the mountaineer, by the lessons of his past if by nothing else, has every right to be suspicious of anybody's doing anything for him. His history has been one of being "done out of" by fast-talking outsiders who have often stripped him of his very means of livelihood. He therefore tends to play it safe, to be ultraconservative, to be reluctant to accept any changes (for they will probably be for the worse), to reject what the world tries to thrust upon him.

It has always been interesting to me to listen to politicians or businessmen or clergymen who have come out of this reference-group background, as they speak to persons still within the reference-group society. They invariably say, somewhere near the beginning of their talk, something like, "Now I'm just a country boy myself," and then go on to use two or three local idioms that would tend to bear them out. It is as though they were saying, "You can trust me, you see. I'm just like you."

Because he tends to take everything very personally, the mountaineer is offended by the smallest hint of criticism. He is quite critical of his friends and cannot believe that others are not critical of him. It was interesting to be in the Southern Appalachians at the time a national magazine published an article about some of the problems of one of the Appalachian states—poverty, unemployment, substandard housing, and the like. The reaction was immediate and intense. These criticisms of some obviously objective realities were taken angrily even by those who were the poor and the unemployed and were living in substandard housing! And one of the state newspapers responded by sending a reporter to the city where the magazine was published to find examples of the same conditions there, printing pictures to prove them. This counterattack, which is what it was,

was highly applauded by the citizenry, as if to say, "You criticized us, and we got back at you." The fact that the paper's findings were beside the point of the original article was not considered. Personal retaliation was the answer that satisfied.

5.
The Mountaineer and the Community

THE middle class traveler, as he journeys through rural Appalachia, is not likely to be favorably impressed with much that he sees. He will observe rows of coal-camp houses with peeling paint; elsewhere, unpainted, weather-stained houses set on blocks or posts (allowing the chickens or house pets some shelter and escape), perched on the hillsides or back from the creek banks; the front porch with its ever occupied rocking chairs or a swing, and children everywhere. In the visitor's eyes the well-kept garden patches and the picturesque narrow footbridges swinging precariously across the creeks in front of the houses cannot make up for the dumps of trash spread everywhere. But despite the sameness of the features noted by the traveler, each type of Appalachian community has distinct characteristics. Coal-mining camps have a different personality from rural farm communities, and a home-owners' community differs markedly from a renters' or squatters' community. The county seat is often almost another world in comparison to any of these; yet the folk culture persists regardless of living arrangements.

As we speak of the mountaineer and the community, however, it must be remembered that for the person in the folk-culture stratum of mountain society, reference-group activity satisfies the need for action, fellowship, and purpose. Thus the community is actually unnecessary to his life except on a very impersonal level; he uses what he needs from the community, ignores the rest, and finds no reason for further community support—unlike the middle class person, who participates in the community and its activities because he shares its values and goals and finds that the organizations of the community further his own purposes.

THE RURAL MOUNTAINEER

Thousands of persons in the mountains still live a life of isolation. These are the families farthest up the hollows, where the creek bed may often serve as the road, in the coves that extend for miles up the twisting valleys, and out on the tops of the mountain ridges. These folk have but occasional contact even with their neighbors, who may well be their own kin. They may not take even a weekly newspaper. The children, however, usually do get to school fairly regularly. In a classroom they can generally be spotted by their head-hanging shyness, their "on-the-outside-looking-in" quality. It is these families—isolated by distance, by lack of roads, and by choice—that most clearly display the characteristics of the folk culture.

They have no community life as such or life outside their very limited family group. The church, which is usually the only organized group nearby, is ignored. Contacts with those outside the reference group are on the most occasional and superficial level—a visit to the nearest store for groceries and mail, a trip to the doctor in an emergency, a rare excursion to a nearby commercial center. The isolated family has as little to do with outsiders as possible, and it expects no interference in its own affairs. Whether the husband farms or works in the mines, his main interests are at home with his family, and he returns there immediately after work.

Attempts to induce such a family to participate in affairs outside their small world meet with repeated rebuffs. Children and youths who wish to share in activities away from home receive little encouragement from their parents. They may even be forbidden to participate, with the excuse that the parents want to keep them close to home so they can keep an eye on them. Those who would broaden the life of this family and enable its members to relate more positively to the world must come as friends who can be trusted. These folk are nonsocial, recognizing no social compact beyond the basis of personal friendship—and even so, each is still suspicious of all others. One of our staff workers who has lived fourteen years in a small rural community says that only now are some of these families beginning to have enough confidence in her to speak freely of personal matters and to ask her counsel. They are virtually impossible to organize into groups and are traditionalistic in the extreme. There are great numbers of these families, and the fact that they must be reached on a person-to-person basis presents one of the major challenges to groups working for the betterment of life in the mountains.

THE RURAL COMMUNITY

All through the mountains one finds small settlements or villages, varying from a few houses and a combination general store, post office, and gas station to a larger town with several stores. These communities are trading centers for the area around them and are generally found in places where the land is still owned by private persons. Much of Appalachia is owned by great land companies, and where this is the case the rural community is less common, being found only on small holdings of private land where the original owner held out against the companies.

These rural communities or small towns usually have a kind of "assorted" look to them. The houses, from the common four rooms heated with coal stoves or fireplaces to quite modern ones, are built anywhere there is land enough. The stores may be anything from converted houses to large buildings with plate-glass windows. Outside house paint is not often a best-selling item in the stores, although inside paint is used in great quantities. Interestingly enough, there are probably few empty houses in these towns; when families leave, others from the more rural areas move in. These will probably be members of one or more of the family groups already living in the town.

What happens person-to-person in these communities is more important to the inhabitants than what is happening in the community as a whole. Where the houses are strung along the highway only one deep, there is a further hindrance to the sense of "community," for one has only two neighbors, one on either side, and the mountain goes up at the back door. The store that houses the post office becomes the communications center in a very unstructured (but efficient) way. The store owner knows pretty well what is going on in the community—who has found work, which families are in real need, who can be counted on if there is a job to do. Sooner or later he sees most everybody, and in these contacts the community and personal news is spread.

There are usually at least two churches, no matter how small the town, and each church is attended by a particular family or reference group. There is little cooperation between them. In fact, the division of the community by church lines is, as a rule, complete. Because the churches are small, intense competition for members goes on between them, further reducing the possibility of cooperative community action.

The nearest thing to community life beyond the reference group may well be the PTA which includes for the most part those persons who are upwardly mobile in each reference group. This organization is often simply a money-raiser for the school, trying to get inside toilets installed, or buying a projector, or keeping the lunch program going.

THE COMMERCIAL CENTER AND COUNTY SEATS

The commercial center presents a different picture. The visitor is surprised to find a community with only a small resident population having two or three supermarkets and a number of modern stores where appliances, furniture, and clothing are tastefuly displayed. In this small town there may well be a bank, a jeweler or two, two florists, two drugstores, a large dime store, several clothing stores, perhaps a bakery, and a number of eating places and taverns. This is the shopping center for several thousand people who come in from the hollows and the coal camps. When the coal mines were booming, every weekend seemed like a carnival, with crowds jamming the streets and stores.

As the mining economy has dwindled, several of the stores have closed. It is more common now to see the streets filled but once a month, and then with slow moving, mud-spattered old cars, pickup trucks, and jeeps filled with children and babies—it is the day that people come to cash their welfare, unemployment, or disability checks. For many mountain folk this is the only venture to town. Without the business these many small checks provide, many more town stores would have to close.

These towns are usually incorporated. There are several service clubs; fraternal organizations such as Masons, Odd Fellows, Moose, and Eastern Star; an American Legion post; a hired policeman or two, and a volunteer fire department. The organizations either are joined by those who have found some mobility away from the person orientation of the reference group, or else they become almost an extension of the reference group itself. In some cases, their chief function seems to be to provide a hangout for the men, since male recreations and activities are very limited. The typical mountaineer, however, is a nonjoiner, or—even a stronger word—an antijoiner. Aside from the women's auxiliaries of the fraternal groups, women's organizations are more likely to center in the church and school.

The major commercial and political center in much of the mountain area is the county-seat town. The courthouse group wields great influence throughout the county, since the government is frequently the biggest business, with the school system getting the lion's share of funds. The presence of this political and economic power draws people and business from all over the county.

THE COAL CAMP

The coal camp presents a much different picture from any of the above communities. It is named appropriately— a "camp"—a temporary community whose very spirit betrays the sense of its limited and uncertain existence, even though the mine may have worked steadily for a generation or more. A person who has lived more than twenty years in such a camp still speaks of "home" as the place where he grew up. Since the camp's existence is entirely dependent upon the mine, its whole life revolves around the routine of the whistles, the shifts, the trains, and the tipple.[1]

Life as it was lived in the traditional coal camp would strike most of us as strange indeed. Because the company owned the whole community, the community danced to the

[1] See Harry Caudill, *Night Comes to the Cumberlands* (Boston: Little, Brown and Company, 1963), esp. pp. 113-15, for a graphic description of a coal camp community.

tune of the company's pipe. The miner and his family, if they went to church, did so in a building provided by the company and heard a preacher who was selected and hired by the company and often paid through a compulsory check-off system before the men received their wages. The school building was often provided by the company and so was the teacher. The store was a company store and bound the miners to it through a system of scrip, which was really an advance on next pay day's money. (This much maligned system began as a service to families and ended by entoiling the unwary, because it made credit so easy to get.) If there were movies in town, they were shown in a company-provided building. Water, electricity, coal, and garbage collection (if any) were provided by the company at token cost. If any community improvements were made—sidewalks, recreation fields, road maintenance—they were usually initiated and carried out by the company. Thus, the company did not train, and did not intend to train, the individualistic mountaineer in forms of community organization. Management told him what needed to be done, and, in total dependence, the miner did what he was told.

The miners' union was the only organization to which the men belonged, and even membership in it was not voluntary. In some places these unions were well organized and efficient, representing the men to the company adequately, while in other places they were largely gripe clubs where the miners let off steam to each other against the company. They also provided an instrument of retribution against the company for grievances suffered—in the form of the wildcat strike, a weapon which some locals used so effectively and so often that the company officials threw up their hands and shut down the mine.

When the United Mine Workers gained real power, it, too, issued orders from above, in many respects taking over the

role formerly played by the company. The union now dic-
tated the salaries and pensions of the men, the working conditions (in the form of safety requirements), the vacations,
and even the amount of rent a man could pay per room for
his house. I do not mean to say that the union did not greatly
improve conditions for the miners; it did. My point is that
the personal growth of individuals toward community responsibility was not one of the main aims of the union. It
is interesting to note, however, that some good leadership
did come out of these local unions. Those working with
mountain people who have moved to the city have found
that the men who had membership in the unions are the
ones who by and large are making the best adjustment to
city life.

TRAITS AT WORK IN THE COMMUNITY

Let us turn now to some examples of the mountaineer's
particular characteristics as they show up in his life in the
community. Basically, his individualism is buttressed and
encouraged by the community situation. Since there is seldom enough prosperity in town for one to get a satisfying
share of the wealth, an every-man-for-himself competition is
openly displayed. As each man looks out for himself—and
looks askance at his competitors—he complains somewhat
bitterly that "nobody will work together in this place."

Several years ago, one of the commercial towns with
which I am familiar had been hit hard economically by the
closing of a number of coal mines in the area. A newspaper
from a neighboring city ran a story headlined "BOOM
TOWN TO GHOST TOWN," documenting it with pictures
of some of the stores that had closed and mines that were no
longer working and with comments from men who had lost
their jobs. The article was taken by the town residents and

the merchants as representing them, personally, as down-and-outers. Some of the people were so angry that they organized a protest meeting. Most of the merchants and a number of the other citizens were there. Out of this unusually vocal meeting came two results: (1) a strongly worded protest to the paper stating that things were not as pictured, and (2) a committee whose purpose was to see what could be done to make things better. Since I was known to be interested in the economic affairs of the area, I was asked to serve on the committee. The leading doctor in the town was chosen chairman.

More than sixty persons attended this first public meeting, and about twenty-five came to the second meeting, at which the committee was to report. When the group saw that a long period of cooperative effort would be needed before any progress toward economic renewal could take place, enthusiasm soon died out, even among a number of the committee members, who reflected the fatalistic feeling, "You can't ever do anything good around here. They won't let you." A few of the members—the doctor, a merchant, and I—carried on for about two years, checking on industrial requirements, possible land sites, what other areas had done, and so forth; significantly, none of us was native to the region. The greatest response of the community was to a plan to storm the offices of the state highway commission with the demand that connecting roads be built over the ridges on either side of the valley that hemmed in the town. In this way, it was reasoned, the people on the other side of those ridges (where businesses were also struggling to keep alive in the limping economy) could come over into their town to shop.

In smaller places, the only community action ever taken is a protest to the school board against some act of the local school or a request for something the school needs; a protest to the road commission about the condition of the road; or a visit to the local politicians to get new bridges built or old ones repaired. Beyond this there is an almost complete lack of determined and organized action. The people simply see no need for it and have no knowledge of how to go about it. The working class mountaineer cannot conceive of the community as a whole, as "we." As mountain people see it, problems are solved either by an individual's doing what is necessary for himself alone or by the reference group's doing things for itself or appealing to the politicians to get it done for them. One reason why the mountaineer so readily resorts to those in the power centers to do things for him is that many of his real problems are, indeed, too great for local solution.

In one of the communities where we work, an attractively located coal camp was bought by a private housing group after the mine closed. The houses were painted in gay colors, fixed up in a minimal way, and sold to anyone wanting them. In the transfer of the property, legal transfer of the water supply (a deep well) was overlooked, but for several years people received water as they always had, paying a flat fee. Since the cost was the same no matter how much water a family used, a number of people let leaks in the pipes or dripping faucets go unrepaired, and the strain on the system grew. In addition, a number of persons defaulted on their water bills. Typically, the man who maintained the pumping equipment and collected the fees, as a member of the reference-group society of the town, was unwilling to shut off anybody's water to force payment of the bill. He was even reluctant to suggest that those wasting water fix their constantly running faucets or toilets, since any word of criticism is taken very much to heart. Finally, during a heavy snowstorm, the pump broke down. For a week the community lined up, buckets in hand, to catch water from a pipe draining from a spring on the mountain, while they waited for the weather to warm up enough so that they could work on the pump.

Only at this juncture did the community begin to organize. Under the leadership of our staff minister, who lived in the town, the men of the community worked together for some days tearing down the system and repairing it. Through the minister's efforts, legal transfer of the water system was made to a corporation of property owners. This corporation also began planning for roads, street lights, recreation facilites and such, which the community lacked. Great interest was shown in the new organization, and under the pressure of the crisis the corporation voted to have the local maintenance man suspend service to those who refused to pay or who allowed water to be wasted through broken pipes.

However, the crisis passed. The water system worked again. Within two months the old order prevailed, the enthusiasm for planning other activities and improvements waned, and the unpaid bills began to pile up and breaks in the pipes went unnoticed. When the pump again broke down, there was a renewed flurry of activity and at this writing, five years later, the utilities corporation is still operative only during periods of crisis and only long enough to get water flowing again.

One of the pressing needs in almost every mountain community is for plans and ideas that come from the local people and have their support. Experts in government, business, and community planning constantly emphasize that the solutions to Appalachia's problems must come from the local scene. Yet such planning is the very thing which mountain people find it next to impossible to do. They can react to a situation calling for action, but they have no experience of the value of mere thinking and paper planning and ac-

cepting the responsibility for the value judgments necessary in every community-betterment program. Most of
those who have the ability to think and plan ahead have
already done so, and their planning has taken most of them
out of the mountains.

One need not live long in the Southern highlands before
one can recognize the tremendous force of traditionalism in
the community. Change of any kind is fiercely resisted.
One must use care and patience in preparing a group to
accept the suggestion that things are not as they should be
and some changes are in order. If they once become convinced of their chance of success, however, and do not expect to be let down or made to look foolish, this group will
become just as strongly attached to their new opinion.

For example, an adult group in one of our churches was
studying the social concerns of the Old Testament prophets,
which led to a discussion of the need to be socially concerned today. The group drew up a list of social conditions
about which they felt the church in their own area should
be concerned. Among these were the tremendous waste of
money by families whose breadwinners were coal miners, the
lack of recreation facilities for all ages, but especially for
men, and the lack of a disposal system for garbage and
trash. When it came to "what can we do," the group decided
to send a list of their concerns to the newspaper. Under
the prodding of the pastor they decided to address themselves to the trash situation. Here, they felt, was something
that certainly needed doing and could at least be looked into.

As things stood, each family had its own dump over the
river bank in front of its house. Heaps of stinking refuse,
old cans, bottles, bedsprings, and cartons made the banks
of every stream look like a continuous trash heap. Swarms
of flies covered the refuse, and a mass of rats grew fat on it.
The bridges of the area were nicknamed "garbage tipples,"
as families threw their refuse over the side into the water

or onto the bank. Tin cans tinkled down the streams day and night, and small boys spent enjoyable hours throwing rocks at floating bottles. A drive up the hollow on a warm summer evening was enough to discourage the strongest stomachs.

Those who lived in the area had grown accustomed to this and did not even seem to see it. Those who traveled through could see little else, and wondered how and why a people with so little to do could not have found the time to exhume themselves from the mounting piles of trash. The high waters of spring were the only collection system. As the waters rose to the tops of the banks, the junk was washed away, along with the topsoil of the hillsides and the sludge of the strip mines. Then began again the ugly accumulation of summer, fall, and winter, awaiting the next "collection."

This was the situation which the group decided to tackle. First, the assistance of the county sanitarian was enlisted, although he lived over the mountain some forty miles away. Community support was sought through a public meeting in a "neutral" building, the school (to have held the meeting in any one of the seven churches of various denominations in the area would have immediately alienated most of the community). Even so, as might have been expected, little response was elicited, and only those in the initiating church ever came to a meeting. The pastor was named chairman, and a committee made arrangements with a coal company for land for a dump (sanitary land fill, as the health department sanitarian always insisted), found a dedicated garbage collection man (one can have no idea how necessary this turned out to be) and, with the blessings of the county health department, started the service. It was to cost each household $1.50 per month and would provide two or three jobs in the community.

Reaction was immediate and violent. One would have

thought that the last rights of the citizenry were being snatched away by an evil despot. While it must be said that many families responded gratefully to the service, others fought it with an unbelievable ferocity. "Everybody has always thrown stuff in the creek." "Why should we pay to have it hauled away, when the river will take it away free?" "Nobody is going to tell me——" One property owner even threatened his tenants with eviction if they signed up for the service. Many a morning the collector found his lawn littered with fresh garbage thrown there by irate persons who would not cooperate. For a time, things actually looked worse, since some persons began dumping trash along the roadsides or in the most conspicuous places. Months of firm determination, a few judicious arrests, and innumerable visits by the patient sanitarian were required to convince the residents that the system of collection was for their good and their health, as well as being "the law."

No matter what the proposal, the dead hand of traditionalism always has life enough to slap it down. "No city feller [change is almost always a "city" idea] is gonna make us over." "You can't make country people into city folk" (and don't you try it). In fact, all the aspects of personality which tend to make the mountaineer unique also tend to make him an anachronism in our interrelated, interdependent society. Whereas a middle class society finds a good part of its being in working for such objectives as community beautification, cultural facilities, or a new health center and its members are easily recruited for groups having such aims, the mountaineer is not only unable to carry out the plans but is baffled by the concept. This inability of persons within the folk culture to conceive of the community in its corporate nature is one of its great weaknesses. As Kephart observes, "There is no such thing as a community of mountaineers. They are knit together, man to man, as friends, but not as a body of men. . . . Our men are almost incapable of concerted action. . . ."[2] Even fair-sized settlements are likely to be only interrelated local reference groups, with no sense of the community as a whole. Where a commercial town is formed, the ties between persons are less personal and the possibility of community action for achieving object goals is more real. Perhaps it is from these less personal towns and cities that the great movement for Appalachia's help must first come. Perhaps it is here that the middle class "caretaker," who almost automatically thinks in such general terms as community structure, community spirit, and community projects, can best work.

[2] Horace Kephart, *Our Southern Highlanders* (New York: Outing Publishing Co., 1913), p. 310.

6.

The Mountaineer and the Outside World

B Y "outside world" I mean all the persons, groups, and
forces which act in the mountains but are not an indigenous part of mountain society. This outside world includes
the educational system, the government on every level except local, the personnel of the railroads and the coal and
land companies, the doctors, the social workers from the
public-welfare office, the educated ministers and mission-
aries, the state police—all those who do not really "belong"
by nature in the mountains. These organizations and the persons who represent them are often looked upon with hostility and suspicion, for they are regarded as wishing to take
some kind of advantage of mountain people. Men are generally more hostile toward these agencies than women,
partly because of their lack of social experience and skills
and partly because they have had fewer contacts with such
groups. These agencies can all be expected to treat the
mountaineer in object-oriented ways. If, by chance, one of
them treats him in a person-oriented fashion, the mountaineer, while still suspicious, reacts much more warmly
and openly. This gulf between the mountaineers and social
agencies of all sorts is a huge obstacle.

THE WORLD OF WORK

For the mountaineer, work has never been particularly
enjoyable. It was a necessity. He did not plan to enter a

particular kind of occupation because he liked it—he worked at whatever there was to do because he had to make a living. The concept of choosing a vocation, becoming trained in that field, and traveling wherever it called him was—and is—largely foreign to the mountain boy. The idea that people can actually enjoy work, or that it can be an outlet for creativity or bring fulfillment, makes little sense to the mountaineer. One works to live, and for no other reason. Work means hard physical labor, and the mountaineer can work very hard for long hours at a stretch. And work in timber, coal mines, and hillside fields is indeed hard. The mountaineer believes that man has been forced to earn his bread by the sweat of his brow since God put Adam and Eve out of the Garden, and work that does not require such effort is hardly considered to be real work at all. Those who have white-collar jobs are thought to be doing less than manly work. The mountaineer cannot imagine what a full-time social worker or church pastor can possibly be doing with his time, since he doesn't work. On a number of occasions I have heard words of approval when I, a pastor, have joined with men of the church and community in doing manual labor. "At last," they seemed to be saying, "we know he can really work." If anyone going to the mountains to serve is the least bit sensitive on this point, he will find that he will drive himself unmercifully, trying to prove to the people that he is really working very hard.

The coal miner is fiercely proud of his skill as a coal miner, although he suspects that his occupation is not highly rated. I have often taken groups to various mines to see the work as it goes on outside the mine entrance (few mines allow visitors inside), and in every single case the reception by the men has been very warm and cordial. They are pleased to have outsiders see how they must work for a living, and will spend a great deal of time explaining every detail, even though they get behind in their own jobs in doing so. I recall the deep admiration I once heard a group of miners express for Eleanor Roosevelt, because she had once actually gone down into a mine to see how the men worked. I remember, too, the first time there was a strike after I moved to the mountains. Even though it meant hardship for his family if it continued very long, one miner at least was glad for the strike. "A little blow-out [strike] don't hurt nothin'. A coal miner ain't nobody till he goes on strike, then ever'body's lookin' at him."

Few families want their sons to be coal miners like their fathers, because they themselves have almost always been poor. The work is dangerous and uncertain, and nowadays there are few jobs available in the good mines. The coal miner expects to be on the bottom of the employment heap, and he expects to be laid off. Even when he moves to the city, he is still on the bottom of the ladder, expects to be laid off, and lives with the attitude that everybody is "down on the poor man" (himself).

Because work's only purpose is earning a living, the mountaineer when unemployed has a different attitude toward unemployment insurance from that middle class leaders envisioned when they set up such payments in the law. The thought was that such insurance would be looked on only as a temporary assistance between jobs. Few middle class persons think of it as anything more than that. It is just to tide one over between jobs—a man should take only what he needs of it. The mountaineer, however, sees this insurance as a legal substitute for work for the entire period that it comes to him. How often, when speaking with a mountain man just after he has been laid off and asking what he is going to do now that his job played out, one will receive the answer, "Well, I don't have to worry none or look for a job for six months, 'cause my unemployment will be coming in that long." Since all you work for, anyway, is the money, and you can get the money legally another way, why work? To many middle class persons such an attitude seems almost immoral; yet from the viewpoint of the mountaineer it is quite natural and makes good sense.

The fact that in the mines there is set pay for every job and the new man gets the same pay as the veteran is satisfactory to most men. Nor does pay vary much among the jobs. This kind of leveling fits the reference-group way of life. The desire to "get ahead" on a job, to be promoted to a job of more responsibility or status, is not there. The Protestant ethic of "work hard, save, get ahead" or the idea of work as a vocation from God are foreign to the mountaineer's understanding. His experience does not confirm them. For him, work is simply the expenditure of time and energy in order to make a living and, if possible, to make life outside the job more pleasurable. Work is to make money to spend on oneself and one's friends.

Until the advent of automation, the only qualifications a man needed were a strong back, willingness to work hard, and the courage to face the hazards of mining or timber work. The whole idea of being trained for a job, or of getting education in advance of even being on the job market, is quite new. Though it will be difficult, it is necessary for the whole mountain society to shift the gears of its thinking about such training as the age of manual labor disappears.

In the process of helping some unemployed families find jobs outside the area, through the resettlement program of the church parish, we discovered considerably more illiteracy among the men than we had realized existed. One man in his mid-thirties was offered a job driving a soft drink truck in a city. The church there would help him find housing, get his family moved and settled, and in every other way possible help to relocate him. The man, unemployed, forced to move within a month because the coal camp where he lived was being torn down, refused the job. On closer investigation, we found that he had checked with the soft drink man who came to the local store and had discovered that he would have to figure up and write out bills for each customer as he delivered the orders. This he could not do. He had been sickly when small and had never gone beyond the first few grades in school. When asked why he had not made known his inability before, since, some way could surely have been found to teach him to read and write, he replied that while in the mines he had not needed to know so he hadn't bothered to learn.

In middle class America, by contrast, work has been elevated to a position of being almost an end in itself. A man is described by the work he does—he's a drill-press operator, he's a teacher, he's a shop foreman—and he finds the chief meaning of his life in relation to his work. In other words, man is to serve industry, and he drives himself ever faster to meet the needs of industries which are filled with yet faster moving machines. It is almost a case of "we live in order to work," while the mountaineer's philosophy is "we work in order to live." He feels no responsibility to work. I know men who have actually quit their jobs in the city and returned to the mountains because the factories expected them to be there every single day. When these men took a few days off in the spring for fishing, or in the fall for hunting, or just wanted a rest from the pace for a day or two, the company expressed disapproval. "Men are to serve the system," industry seemed to be saying to these men, and this philosophy the mountain man had no intention of buying.

It is still common for a man working in the city to return home to the mountains during times of crisis or death in his family—not necessarily his immediate family. When a cousin or someone else not too closely related dies, the man may take off the better part of a week to be present at the funeral. This family duty is so important that even though there is the chance that he may lose his job, he goes home anyway. Or young men may take off a number of days to come home to help the family with spring plowing. On industry's part, this makes the mountain man seem undependable. From the other side, the mountaineer does not understand a way of life which elevates work above what he feels to be the real human values.

Because work is part of the outside world, there is seldom a sense of cooperation between the coal miner and his employers. Often a kind of hostility is shown toward the company: the men waste time on the job and use the machinery roughly. Toward the land companies that own the great tracts on which the mountaineer hunts, contempt is often expressed. Somehow the land company epitomizes the hostile outside world. Stealing trees and illegally mining coal seams is not unheard of, and the mountaineer starts fires and lets them rage through the mountains for weeks on end, caring little that the game he wants to hunt is destroyed, the trees that he would be hired to cut are scarred, and the ground cover, which preserves the water level, is destroyed. His attitude toward any property, including his own, is far from a loving and caring one. I will not say this has always been so, but in recent years this attitude has certainly been growing.

EDUCATION

Almost every mountain child has the opportunity (at least, as we see it) to attend public school. Only in relatively few cases is attendance not possible—where families live on top of the mountains or far up the twisting valleys, remote from schools or school-bus routes. Schools vary from the one-room variety up to modern, centralized systems with hundreds of students. Often long bus rides are necessary, over rough and dangerous roads, but few children do not have the possibility, at least, of having twelve years of public schooling. But they do not always get it. Since the forms of education were imposed from the outside and did not grow up as an expression of the culture, teaching what the mountaineer wanted his children to learn, there has traditionally been a resistance to "book learning." A person was thought well enough educated if he could read and write and count, and "too much" schooling was thought to be unnecessary and even dangerous—and so was unwanted.

In the past, children were sent to school as early as allowed, but whenever they were old enough to be helpful at home or on the farm or in the mine, they were taken out of school either for a time or for good. Sometimes the girls were needed at home to help their mothers with the smaller ones or to serve as mother substitutes in cases of sickness or disability. School was always secondary to something else. One day, for instance, I picked up a boy thumbing a ride in front of the school. It was several hours before school was to be dismissed, and I asked him whether he had to go to the doctor, or perhaps had been called home because of some emergency. No, he replied, he had gotten an excuse from his father to come home early to help dig potatoes. Since it was Friday, I asked whether he weren't going to do that the next day. "Why no," he said, in a tone which seemed to indicate that I must not be very discerning. "Tomorrow's the start of hunting season."

Parents now want their children to have an education, because they have become increasingly aware that it is necessary; yet they fear that it will separate children from their families or destroy the common level of the reference group. To be educated means to be "uppity" or snobbish, or to feel that one is better than the rest. A young person who has gone off to college may return at vacation time to find his family and reference group asking, in so many words, "Do you think you're better than we are now?" There is almost a fear of an education that goes very far above the community level. A man who could not find a job because of his limited education expressed to me a great deal of hostility against companies which advised him to go back to school and get some basic courses, such as English. "Why do I need more English to get a job?" he stormed. "I can talk all right. What's the difference if I tell him that I ain't got no job and I need the money in plain talk or some fancy way. He knows what I mean—or he should." Education must have immediate and specific application before the mountain man counts it important or necessary. Yet most mountain schools have taught standard college preparatory courses, with little emphasis on crafts or skills. Most of the education has been object oriented, presenting the kind of information that the mountaineer simply does not understand and ideals that he does not share.

In these adult-centered mountain families, separation between adults and children begins about the time the child enters school and increases rapidly. Because the realm of ideas is not his world, the parent lacks interest in the school. Probably there are no books at all in the home, the child has never been read to, and when he begins having trouble with homework he finds little help or encouragement from parents who may actually have had less education than he has. In some cases, adults may revel in the fact that through "just common sense" they can solve arithmetic problems, for example, faster than their children, who use school-taught methods.

Quite common in the mountains is the unspoken attitude

that education is mainly for girls. Most of the teachers are women, and for the boys and men this fact alone smacks of education's being "sissy." As a natural consequence, the best students are girls, the scholastic striving is among them, and they are most likely to go to college. This is unfortunate, for many a mountain boy finds himself at the same disadvantage in life as his father. The women generally have reached a considerably higher education level than the men. It is not uncommon to find a college-trained teacher married to a man who has not even finished high school. Another factor is the action-seeking trait among the boys; coupled with the dullness of daily mountain life, it certainly does not enhance for them the idea of sitting still to listen and learn. Caudill notes that during the early years of school building in the mountains: "[S]uch new schools as the bond issues provided fell prey to athletics to an extent that is difficult to overstate. The miner (and mountaineer) learned quickly to escape from the dreary routines of camp life and coal digging into the exhilaration of a basketball gymnasium or a football stadium, and was far more interested in the hoopla of school sports than in the riddles of grammar and mathematics. His enthusiasm went to the sterile playing fields and his children, imbued with his infectious zeal, sought to emulate his heroes on grid and court."[1]

Motivation for learning is often lacking among both boys and girls. For one thing, educational achievement requires the ability to handle concepts and ideas, to concentrate on the study at hand to the exclusion of other concerns. The mountain child's training in home and reference group has not schooled him to do this well. The reference-group society trains its members to be sensitive to people rather than to ideas. Words are used not to express ideas but to impress

[1] Harry Caudill, *Night Comes to the Cumberlands* (Boston: Little, Brown and Company, 1963), p. 25.

people, and argument proceeds by the use of anecdotes rather than by commonsense forms of logic. I recall a mountain man's description of the way a particular church group used the Bible. The group, he said, would take a verse here, one there, to build up its own case. The man, in very personal, anecdotal style, remarked that they were "making a saddle to fit their horse." Very plain and clear, yet very difficult to square with ideas of logic, math, or science. It is extremely difficult, for example, to keep any study or discussion group on the subject at hand or on the problem to be solved. The mountaineer is simply not interested in abstract ideas, or in intellectual fine points, or in learning for the sake of learning.

Reference-group life, with its impulsive approach to child rearing, its stress on action rather than routine, the competitive nature of its conversation (where several people may be talking at once), encourages a short attention span. This inability to concentrate for long periods, combined with the inability to see the value of learning that cannot be applied immediately, hinders the mountain child in his education. Certainly it is not lack of intelligence that makes him fall behind his city counterparts. Mountain children, like children everywhere, are quick to learn, but they are much quicker to catch feelings than ideas. The problem is that our educational system is based on ideas, not on feelings.

Much of the parents' laxness toward their children's education simply results from lack of experience on their part. How can a family know the value of a college education or trade-school training when they have seen so little evidence of its worth in their own lives or in their communities? In many a mountain community, the only college-educated person is the school teacher, and unfortunately he is so underpaid (a subtle evaluation of his presumed worth to the community), and often so little thought of, that his place in the world is no incentive to further education. It is to the credit of such teachers that so many of the young people who do go out to get education do so in the field of teaching. Yet how can parents in these isolated valleys know all about the possibilities for careers in aviation, law, business, art, music, engineering, or real estate? The chances are they have never even known anybody in these fields or perhaps don't even know that they exist. Indeed, many a mountain youth has never even seen a large factory, let alone known the kinds of jobs within them, until he leaves home to apply for work in one. It is incredible how immobile large segments of our mountain population can be, while living in the midst of the most mobile society that has ever existed. Mountain boys and girls simply must have experiences that will acquaint them with the "outside" world to which most of them will be forced to migrate—and the educational system must help provide these experiences.

For years, mountain-bred and mountain-taught teachers have been teaching mountain children. I admire tremendously those young people who break out of their home patterns to attend teachers colleges in their home state, and then return to teach near home. Their pay is low, and they have low status in the community, few supplies and books to work with, and multitudes of poorly equipped students in overcrowded rooms. There is real devotion in such a career.

Despite all this, my contention is that we are all more or less blind to our own culture. Mountain-bred and mountain-taught teachers find it too easy to perpetuate the ingrown and experienceless training characteristic of mountain schools. The Southern Appalachians desperately need teachers trained and reared in other cultures, with other experiences and often broader training. Perhaps even a teacher exchange, using mountain and city teachers, would be useful. Too often the mountain school system becomes a "closed shop," composed of a staff of teachers who have been trained in the same system, brought up in the same culture, and molded by the same forces as the children they seek to teach. Instead of challenging and stimulating the children, such a system simply perpetuates itself—and it cannot hope to prepare its youth for life in our American society. To be sure, it would be a mistake to go too far in the other direction. Public schools need both the direction and the understanding of the teacher who knows the feeling and the structure of the person-oriented reference-group society of the mountains as well as the outlook of persons from elsewhere who are not blind to the culture.

A broad educational program will probably not come about soon. Good teachers, wherever trained, can earn much better salaries in more stimulating surroundings than Southern Appalachia. Finally, many a mountain county school system is set up on a political basis, or a person-to-person hiring system. Persons wanting to come into the mountains to teach very often find it difficult to get in— especially in the school systems where outside help is most needed.

POLITICS

In view of the mountaineer's individualism, his person-orientation, his inability to organize and work together, his disinterest in leadership because it jeopardizes his position within the reference group, one would think he would completely reject all political connections. Add to these elements the religious factor—the other-wordliness that rejects involvement in the "evil" world and counsels a man to strive for the heavenly kingdom—and the picture would seem to become even clearer. And quite mistaken!

Numbers of mountain people, in fact, are greatly interested in politics. There is as surely a "political season" as
there is a baseball season. In a county with which I am
acquainted more than twenty candidates entered a recent
primary for four legislative seats. Families put signs for
various candidates in their windows and tack them on their
porches or fence posts, and plaster their cars with stickers.
It is a time of excitement, of extra visiting, of person vying
with person. The rallies, the parades, the speeches, the
name-calling all spell action, and people thrive on it. It is
a respite from the boredom of life.

Election day has a festive spirit. Crowds of people stand
about the polling places the greater part of the day making
predictions, discussing the candidates, or trying to convince
the uncertain. (In a local town election, where the issues
were unusually pointed and heated, 96 percent of the regis-
tered population turned out to vote.) Vote buying is still
fairly common, so interested are many to see that their candi-
date wins. At primary time in 1963, the liquor commission of
one mountain state ordered a quantity of pints of whisky for
their retail stores—a pint being the going price for a vote.
Newspaper comment on this fact brought immediate and
heated denial that vote buying had anything to do with
the order, but the fact remains that great quantities of this
particular-size bottle are used at no other time.

The mountaineer's individualism and person-orientation
team up to lead him into politics so that he can get favors
for his own area, people, and reference group. He conceives of government processes in terms of personal relationships, much like those in his reference group. He sees
the actions of government not in terms of general order or
of law but in terms of the personal whims of each official.
Thus, government agencies are closely identified with the
persons who run them. If those in power are not person-

oriented, he sees them as enemies or as corrupt in their dealings toward him.

The idea that government officials must follow rules of good business or good politics, based not on personal morality but on concepts of order, efficiency, and fairness, to all is difficult for the mountaineer to understand. Administrative channels are considered "the run around." He does not really believe in representative government, for he does not sufficiently trust other people. His idea is that elected officials are subject to him, not that they possess a rightful delegated authority. The mountaineer judges government as good or bad by the extent to which its policies serve him. There is much sectional fighting for control of the political offices at stake, each district being determined to get its fair share of the favors. Each section of the county or the state tries jealously to guard its rights and powers against other sections. If one side of the county gets a new road or school or public building, the other side immediately concludes that somebody bribed the officials, or misappropriated the money, or betrayed the voters. Many a man runs on a "Christian" ticket, trying to convince the voters to elect him because he is a "good" man, as against all those thieves now in office. Since everybody else in the government is corrupt (read "have not served him well enough to improve his lot"), he is going to see that things get cleaned up and that his district gets a larger slice of the melon. In this sense, politicians are not altogether part of the outside world but may be seen to be, as Gans suggests, "ambassadors to the outside world."[2]

Once a person is elected, be it justice of the peace, constable, school-board official or whatever, he immediately attempts to run a person-oriented office. Naturally, poor

[2] Herbert J. Gans, *The Urban Villagers* (New York: Free Press of Glencoe, 1962), pp. 163-80.

government results. Sectionalism is encouraged. Overall planning and strategy is neglected and piecemeal projects are undertaken. Political figures find themselves having to do personal favors, and government based on personal whims finds itself unable to make objective decisions that could lead to progress.

It is interesting to note that whereas every other area of life has closed the doors of opportunity to the mountaineer, only politics has allowed him some freedom to act, some opportunity for achievement. In this realm, he feels that his work is not wasted but that there is in fact the promise of a new order of things for himself and his family.

MEDICAL CARE

In another area of life, the mountaineer must also go to the outside world for help—when serious or prolonged illness strikes. Most small ailments are treated at home by patent medicines and home remedies, which are a kind of folk medicine that often turns out to be amazingly effective. Various kinds of treatments using teas, roots, berries, turpentine, honey, and lye have served the mountain man and his family for generations, from the days when doctors were absolutely unavailable. He learned early that he had to fend for himself. But when serious illness strikes nowadays, he must turn to the outside world for help—outside because there are no doctors within the reference group structure, although a few mountain boys have been trained and have returned, and because mountaineers do not hold the same conceptions of illness as do doctors.

The mountain man is resigned to seeing an outside doctor because he is forced to, not because he believes wholeheartedly in the practices of modern medicine. He has a negative attitude toward doctors, hospitals, and the whole process of medical care. One family was relating to us how their child had "double pneumonia." They were forced to take him to the doctor, who prescribed a series of three antibiotic shots. After the boy had received two shots, on successive days, the mother declared that since he seemed to be getting better she wasn't going to take him back for the third. "I hate for him to have too many shots," she said. In other words, the less contact with modern medicine the better!

Many mountaineers turn to the old general practitioners still living in the area rather than to new clinics and doctor's offices. These old doctors can speak the language of the people; they impart a feeling of confidence, while younger doctors do not. The approach of the older doctors is in sharp contrast to a middle class doctor's practice, where the patient is treated as an active partner in the cure, can be informed about diagnoses and methods of care, and may at times even be told that the doctor is uncertain about the diagnosis or the treatment. The mountain doctor cannot betray any lack of knowledge or certainty, but must assume a dogmatic and omniscient command of the situation, hoping thereby to get his patients to follow his prescriptions.

Mountain people are often afraid of illness and postpone seeing the doctor for fear he will find something wrong with them. Many of them are frightened of hospitals and are suspicious of hospital care and treatment. I have heard people express the most morbid ideas about hospitals, as they recount terrible mistakes and failures of which no modern hospital could be guilty. They charge the hospitals with a lack of care or concern for patients, and even go so far as to say with apparent utter belief that hospitals really try to kill people rather than help them get well. Because hospitals must treat persons in an other than person-oriented way, the mountain patient believes that the nurses and doctors and attendants cannot really be caring for them as they should. Thus members of a patient's family will take turns keeping round-the-clock vigils, to make sure he gets the kind of care he needs and to make sure the doctors and nurses do not try to do something wrong.

The doctor himself is often the butt of cruel jokes or the subject of uninformed criticism. He is criticized if he does not make house calls for the most trivial of reasons, and he is criticized for charging a higher fee if he does make them. He is thought to be getting rich off the sufferings of other people. It is believed that he really does not know much about medicine and that cures are more the work of good drugs or the good Lord than of the doctor's skill. Because the doctor is not in the reference group, he is looked on with suspicion.

For the doctor, establishment of a reasonable doctor-patient relationship is often incredibly difficult. He fiinds it hard to get any kind of logical description of the illness out of the patient unless he becomes familiar with the terms used in the area. If TV commercials give one a bizarre idea of the workings of the human body, the mountaineer can top them all! Descriptions of ailments and operations are most original and unusual, and doctor's words describing disorders are often twisted into unrecognizable forms. A man once told me that the reason another person had died was that he had no kidneys left; they had disappeared. I had to mull that over some time before it dawned on me that the doctor had said that they were "gone"—not functioning any more—not that they had disappeared. My wife tells of an occasion when she sympathetically listened to a woman tell about her little boy, who had been "running off." My wife kept trying to find out what made the boy unhappy enough to do that. The dawn came when she discovered that "running off" is a term for diarrhea. If the boy had been running away from home, as my wife thought, the woman would have said that he was "slipping off." Other common complaints are a "beeled head," "low blood," and "nerves."

The mountaineer's attitudes toward medicine are much influenced by his person-orientation. Because the medical profession cannot treat him in such a way, personally sharing his ills empathetically, he feels that object-oriented doctors, hospitals, clinics, and nurses are using him. Because he is an action seeker, he seeks medical care only in response to crisis. Little thought is given to preventive medicine or preventive measures. The purpose of the dentist is to pull aching teeth, not to provide the cleaning and the filling and the care necessary to preserve teeth. Many a mountain mother-to-be receives no prenatal medical care or advice. When the pains start, she is rushed to the hospital. When one thinks of the almost complete lack of opportunity and money in the past, there is no need to wonder how such a "crisis" approach to medicine developed. In some areas close to us, severe epidemics of polio broke out several years ago. The incidence of polio in our immediate area was high enough to frighten many adults, for sickness among small children is to the mountaineer the worst kind of all. Yet, when free oral poliovaccine clinics were held in the area, a number of families did not go, even though transportation was provided for them. They simply could not see the value of preventive medicine—even for their children.

What is said about sickness in general is all the truer for mental illness; the mountaineer cannot accept it. "Poor nerves" or "worn-out nerves" are blamed for such disturbances. The psychiatrist's care can be accepted only if he is called a "nerve doctor." The whole subject of mental illness is simply foreign to mountain people.

The sense of fatalism that runs through all of life in the

mountains comes into prominent play in medicine. For instance, I have seen diabetic persons go to the doctor for treatment, then completely disregard any medicine or diet prescriptions they received, saying that it really wouldn't help much anyway because they wouldn't die before their time and nothing they could do would prolong their lives. It has been this sense of fate (although it is not really fate, for it is not a conspiring of impersonal forces but a pre-arranged plan of God Himself) that has been the cushion for the mountaineer's heart against the rough times of his life—the death of the children, the killing of the husband in the mines or woods, the senseless accident with the ax, the death in childbirth of the wife.

7.

The Mountaineer and the Church

THE religious heritage of the Southern Appalachian people
has been pictured as 'leftwing Protestantism.' Its characteristics include puritanical behavior patterns, religious
individualism, fundamentalism in attitudes toward the Bible
and Christian doctrine, little distinction between clergy and
laity, sectarian concepts of the church and its mission, re-
vivalism, informality in public worship, and opposition to
central authority of state or church."[1] This description of
religion in the Southern Appalachians is almost exactly opposite from the traditions of much American Protestantism
and of the clergy trained in seminaries. It is hardly surprising that many dedicated young men from the cities and
towns of mainstream America find themselves completely
frustrated as they try to minister in the religious situation
of Appalachia. Harry Caudill notes that the mountaineers, in
the main irreligious, simply are not joiners of organizations of
any kind except political parties.[2] In some areas the proportion of church membership in the population is below 30
percent, with male membership somewhere around 5 percent and teen-age youth membership falling to the range of
1 to 2 percent.

HISTORIC TENDENCIES

I will not attempt to give more than a brief description of
the religious history of the mountain area. My hope here,

as in the other pages of this book, is to give only enough background to provide some understanding of the situation. Many sections of our country were settled by people who held in common a fairly homogeneous religious heritage— the Puritans in New England, the Quakers in Pennsylvania, the Anglicans in Virginia. Later, during the great immigration periods, the Irish settled in Boston and the Lutherans in the Midwest, and the Italians, Poles, and Jews clustered together in certain areas of the growing cities. The common religious heritage of the immigrants who settled together provided one of the unifying and sustaining forces that helped these newcomers to America to find their places.

On the other hand, the first settlers in Appalachia, who came largely from the lower economic groups, were a diverse lot religiously—Scotch Presbyterians, English Puritans and Separatists, and nonconforming sectarians from various backgrounds.[3] No one church ever developed sufficient strength to draw them together. People were too widely separated and travel was too difficult for a stable ministry to be provided. Trained clergymen on the east coast, already overburdened with the press of the fast-growing population there, were reluctant to travel into the untamed wilds of Appalachia.

Education of the clergy held no more appeal for the mountaineer than did education of his children. Presbyterians, among the few to require seminary training for their ministers, were to split in the mountains over this very issue. On the perennial frontier of Appalachia a man had to work for his living—let not those who led the church be excused

[1] Earl D. C. Brewer, "Religion and the Churches," in *The Southern Appalachian Region: A Survey*, ed. Thomas R. Ford (Lexington: University of Kentucky Press, 1962), p. 201.

[2] *Night Comes to the Cumberlands* (Boston: Little, Brown and Company, 1963), p. 349.

[3] Brewer, p. 201.

from this, cither. So there grew up a host of lay preachers who were farmers or miners or shopkeepers through the week and preachers on Sunday. The gentler world of church-manship never appealed to the man whose life was hard and rugged. When he did "get religion," he found the spirit of the Baptists and the Methodists to be more in keeping with his frontier life. Their preachers were plain folks who spoke in the unlettered tongue he understood. They were fron-tiersmen like him, and their homey ways made them quickly acceptable in his home.

The Baptist form of government, which set up the local church as the only authority and allowed no interference from regional or national bodies, was most compatible with the leveling philosophy of the mountaineer. A kind of lay religion grew up in which each congregation became its own interpreter of the Bible and theology and recognized no new ideas from the outside. The fierce individualism of the moun-taineer carried this spirit to the extreme—every man became his own highest authority. The mountaineer recognizes no experts, religious or otherwise. "Even when a wan-dering preacher found occasion to pass a night in a cabin," says Caudill, "he was likely to find his opinions resented and rejected, because the frontiersman believed that one man knew as much about the road to paradise as an-other."[4]

Fervent religious revivals swept through the region in the 1800s, and the custom continues to this very day. Traveling evangelists on horseback would move from place to place, holding "protracted meetings" in tents and bringing excite-ment and action into the dull life of the mountaineer. Preach-ing would be highly emotional, direct, and fear-filled, as the evangelists sought to convert the sinners to a saving faith. The revival is still today a major form of religious service in

[4] Caudill, p. 25.

the mountains, emphasizing an emotional, episodic, and action-oriented kind of religious experience, thus matching the characteristics of the rest of the mountain man's life.

Before we begin to consider the characteristics of the mountaineer's religion, let it be emphasized that just as a psychologist studies abnormal psychology not because everybody is abnormal but so that he can better understand the nature of all of us, so what is related here does not tell the complete story. I would simply emphasize the "purer" extremes, so that the more normal situation may be better understood against this background.

RELIGIOUS INDIVIDUALISM AND SELF-RELIANCE

The Southern Appalachians are full of small, struggling churches. "In 1952, there were nearly twice as many churches per 1,000 population in the Southern Appalachians as in the country as a whole." And the membership of each was little more than one-third the national average.[5] In the area of my own work there are about 100 churches for 20,000 people, which means that if every single person (including infants) was a church member, the average size of a congregation would be only 200 persons. When you recall that 20 to 35 percent of the population is nearer the actual figure for church membership, the situation can be seen, from an outsider's point of view, as extreme and even ludicrous.

It is not that mountain people are anti-religious. They talk a great deal about religion, in fact. It is one of the real live issues of the day. One can easily get a conversation going on the subject of the Bible or prayer or some theological question. Religious arguments are part of the standard talk in every reference group. Persons who never go near the church speak openly about how they hope the good Lord will deal

5 Brewer, p. 210.

with them, or how He has spared them. Many a section crew in the mines begins its day with prayer, even though only the one who leads may have a Christian commitment. Community meetings, too, are often opened with prayer. Until the Supreme Court decisions against religious ceremonies in the schools, a great number of mountain schools had daily devotions, prayers, and Bible study, even though a very small number of the teachers or pupils had any church connections.

The extreme individualism of the mountaineer, however, does not encourage him to participate in the church, much less to join it as a member. As in his relationship to the community, he does not understand the concept of the church as a corporate community of believers, nor does he see the need for such an entity. Religion is an individual matter, just as are his other affairs. The purpose of the church in his life has seldom been other than to win souls to faith in God in a very personalistic way. He simply has no experience or concept of the church's having a mission in the world which might require the faithful to work together. A number of persons claim to be Christians, yet oppose joining a church or even becoming closely associated with one: "No, I ain't churchy, I go to them all. They're all good." To join a particular church would mean that a man would have to help on a routine, regular basis and attend faithfully. But the mountaineer knows that in any group tensions and disagreements are likely to occur. Since he has little skill in resolving these without anger, he prefers to remain free of groups. He wants to be able to sample revivals and services in order to find one that meets his own felt needs. Such an approach to religion is more than likely to degenerate into finding a church that satisfies only his ego or his whims, and does not help his spiritual growth.

This individualism rejects all forms of discipline in re-

ligion. If a church does not suit the mountaineer by preach-
ing what he wants to hear in the way he wants to hear it or
does not give him enough opportunity to assert himself and
be heard, he will quit and go somewhere else. If he is a
strong personality, he may even form his own church, where
he is the minister and "boss," perhaps erecting a building in
his front yard and naming the church after his family. I
know of a case in which a group of such disgruntled egotists
came together and ordained each other, so that they could
go out and start their own congregations with a "Revener"
before their names! The mountains hold a great many of
these "churches," based on the personal desires and feelings
of their members, usually split off from a larger group—ingrown little bodies that pamper their people in order to
keep them coming and thus confirm them in their favorite
prejudices. Up many hollows, churches stand side by side
or across the road from each other, seemingly glaring at each
other and each daring the other to provide an adequate ministry with a handful of people, divided resources, and untrained leadership. The church in Appalachia is, beyond
doubt, the most reactionary force in the mountains.

Accustomed to depend upon himself except in cases of
utmost extremity, the mountaineer turns to God and to the
doctor just about simultaneously. In crises of illness or trouble or when his own death or that of a member of the family
seems imminent, he calls on God. Religion thus is a crutch
for times of trouble but is not of much use in daily life.
Deathbed conversions are still common; in fact, one of the
mountain preacher's solemn duties is to wring a confession
out of every moribund sinner who has not voluntarily "sent
for the preacher."

A desire to live for the highest and best that he knows, a
determination of the will, a reasoning of the mind, or even
the pressure of the community—any of these may impel a

middle class person toward acceptance of faith. These reasons do not convince the mountaineer. Only an extreme crisis or a cataclysmic emotional experience is enough to move him to a public avowal of faith. Through the years the feeling grew that the only way a man can be saved is through an emotional experience which moves him against his will—the revival. Those who come into church membership on confession of faith after a communicant class are scarcely thought to be saved at all.

A "good" revival service with a lively evangelist, enthusiastic singing with heart-rending special music, perhaps accompanied by a guitar, and group prayer where all the faithful gather at the front and pray aloud at the same time, can create an atmosphere of tense expectancy. Soon some will "get happy" and begin "speaking in tongues," as the service provides release for people who have been pent up in the midst of an incredibly dull life. The explosions of emotion which occur in the loud shouting and convulsive crying bring release to many who have no recreations, no social outlets, and no creative work to do it for them. G. Norman Eddy notes that one of the fundamental needs that such services meet for the emotionally starved is the providing of an acceptable opportunity for emotional expression.[6] Such is the case in city or mountains.

Children, too, are emotionally caught up by the crowd, the singing, and the excitement. Seeing their elders sobbing and crying in front of everyone, children of six and seven go up front to join their parents and be saved, too. Sometimes, however, children see only the humorous side of the experience. I have watched them "playing church" in the school yard during recess. "This is the way Sister Mary does,"

[6] "Store-Front Religion," in *Cities and Churches: Readings on the Urban Church*, ed. Robert Lee (Philadelphia: Westminster Press, 1962), pp. 181-82.

one will say, imitating in a humorous way the jerks and sobs and shouts exhibited the night before at the revival.

For the young people, the revival is more of a social occasion. The girls gather inside the church, the boys outside. When some excitement seems to be taking place, the boys come in; when it abates, they wander out again. It is an entertainment, and often not accepted by the youth as a religious service. Walking the girls home afterward makes the standing around worthwhile.

Even though converted, the mountain man still has an "out" that preserves his freedom to continue to live on his own terms. If the emotion which first moved him dies down or the crisis resolves itself (he gets well or the child lives), he "backslides." He simply gives up his faith, returns to his old ways, and is likely to blame it all on the devil. When temptations come, instead of using his faith to overcome them, he backslides. Whenever he does not care to behave as he feels a Christian should, he can backslide: a "sinner" isn't expected to be much. This is a very convenient religion, if not exactly satisfactory for strengthening one's life. A glib acceptance of this escape can strip a man of every bit of discipline and courage and perseverance that religious faith should provide for him. In sum, the mountain man does not become a Christian unless he is "forced" to, and he can back out of his commitment whenever it suits his fancy. His individualism and self-reliance remain intact through it all.

RELIGIOUS TRADITIONALISM AND FATALISM

As might be expected, the religious beliefs of the mountaineer are traditional in the extreme. He clings to the things he believes his fathers clung to—"that old-time religion." Some of his forebears brought with them a strict

Puritan ethic. Even today, the stricter groups hold that social dancing, attending movies or participating in commercial entertainments, wearing cosmetics, jewelry, shorts, or slacks, are decidedly wrong for the Christian. Those who believe that women should wear long sleeves and long skirts and never cut their hair are not increasing, but they are still common. One man told me that he knew he was no longer a Christian when he found himself looking at the ball scores in the paper! In some areas the folk dances which represent the finest of the cultural tradition of the mountains are not acceptable, even when labeled "folk games." Many mountain young people reject the faith of their parents, saying that they don't want to "just sit down and be old, if that is what being a Christian is."

It is important to note that the mountaineer did have good reason to look askance at dancing, ballgames, and other get-togethers. Very often these activities turned into brawls, sometimes serious ones. A group of young boys drinking, with nothing to do and with no restraints from officers of the law, would often erupt into fights, where one or two of them might easily be killed. Even today it is difficult in many communities to have such get-togethers at schools or other public places without trouble brewing. Rather than risk trouble, the ethic of the area labels all such activities as wrong. When a local skating rink opened to serve the youth, such genteel signs as "No Cursing," "No Drinks Allowed," "No Fighting In or Out of the Building," "No Spitting on the Floor," were displayed. A number of the churches nearby immediately had prayer services, asking the Lord to burn down the "den of iniquity," and strictures were uttered against any of their youth's attending. A few good fights, to which the police were called, only confirmed their belief. "You can't have nothin' around here but somebody spoils it fer ever'body," was the prevailing comment. The place closed rather than buck the tide. It is indeed unfortunate that such recreations as might serve Appalachian youth are so closely identified with trouble-making, and so denied them.

Never having been trained in the use of words, or in the understanding of subtle differences between ideas, mountain people have never appreciated anything but a simple literalistic belief in the Scriptures. Something must be right or wrong, black or white, true or false, and they are impatient with the fine points or shades in between.

Simple fundamentalism has provided an uncomplicated answer. As Caudill says, "A people whose only experience for generations had been with a world of hard realities unadorned by the arts, eloquence, or imagination, it was inevitable that their folk churches should be founded upon fundamentalism of the starkest sort."[7] The Bible was all true, all right, and every word could be taken at face value. This outlook has been hammered into mountain minds by preachers in revivals and over radio and TV. There have seldom been trusted persons within the reference-group structure who could help them see beyond this blind acceptance. There is great feeling for "the Book," and multitudes will say, "I believe every word of the Bible from cover to cover," and quote John's curse about adding or taking away (Revelation 22:18-19), but this belief is not based on actual knowledge of "the Book."

For the mountaineer, the Bible is a magical book. He has a respectful reverence for it, but it is a reverence without scholarship or learning. By taking certain passages out of context and misquoting them to suit the purpose in mind, he but reinforces common prejudices. The mere reading of the Bible, even by nonbelievers, is thought to be a righteous act and worthy of godly praise. Such use of the Bible,

[7] Caudill, p. 56.

coupled with the mountaineer's individualism, results in a folk religion, not in a Biblical Christianity. This folk religion is based on sentiment, tradition, superstition, and personal feelings, all reinforcing the patterns of the culture. It is self-centered, not God-centered. Folk prayer becomes a tool to serve *my* needs and to help *me*. The folk church becomes a group whose main purpose is to reiterate the accepted religious ideas and to satisfy personal ego needs, not to bear a witness or do a work for God.

A teacher and choir member I knew, a very faithful member of a church, lost his job in the mines and very soon dropped out of all church activities. Later he explained why: "My religion says that God looks after His own, but He let me lose my job and hasn't helped me find another. If God isn't going to look after me any better than that, I just won't bother with Him, either." The all-pervading folk religion has done a great disservice to mountain people, letting this aspect of their lives—like all the other aspects— be centered in themselves, instead of helping draw them out beyond their own personal concerns.

Dr. Earl D. C. Brewer, a sociologist at Emory University, told of the comment by one of the field workers who assisted him in *The Southern Appalachian Region* section on religion. This graduate student in sociology, a Roman Catholic from Cuba, said to Dr. Brewer that the position of the Protestant Church in Appalachia is much like that of the Roman Catholic Church in Cuba. It is entrenched, socially ineffective, and carries in its teaching the baggage of folk culture which has accumulated over the centuries, from which it cannot separate itself—nor does it try.

The fatalism of the mountaineer leads him to accept an other-worldly and socially passive ethic. Because his hopes have so often been frustrated in this life and because he has never lived with real joy and satisfaction, his eyes and heart have turned to the promises of the future life. Often have I heard a mountain mother tearfully exclaim that "in heaven some day I'll see all my little ones again"; or a man whose health has been ruined by work in the mines declare that "we ain't got no joy here on this earth . . . only heaven's gonna make us happy"; or a father crushed by the poverty that he did not create, and labeled "not worthy to live" by the smallness of his disability check, say that "we'll be rich some day by-n-by." It is almost impossible to relate the poignant longings of a people for a tomorrow of wealth and joy and health in heaven to a society of surpluses and vacations and medical centers.

The other side of the coin of other-worldliness is social passivity: "Ain't no use doin' nothin'. The only thing that can make things right is for the Lord Himself to come." The social action let's-do-something-about-it philosophy of the modern American church is foreign to folk culture Appalachia—as in fact, is any positive and pragmatic approach to any kind of problem. The mountain man's religion is of a piece with his whole outlook on life: it is motivated by fear— the very real, if intermittent, fear of eternal damnation, and the church services are action centered (he finds ordinary religious functions dull).

To work in Appalachia in any field, one must be vitally aware of these deep feelings of mountain people—their long history of failure and loss; their backward stance toward the only security they ever knew; their eager longing for a time and place where things will finally work out well for them for a change, when the reference group will be reunited in heaven. One who has not lived through such abysmal poverty, who has not faced such a deadend life, who has not lived year after long year in the midst of blasted hopes, cannot really understand the eager clutching of this people after the gracious promises of the faith. Those who come to work and to minister must do so with great sympathy for mountain religion. For many it is the only hope, and to destroy it without replacing it with a livelier hope is a great injustice to a people who have already suffered too much at the hands of outsiders.

8.

The Mountaineer and the Future

APPALACHIA has been rediscovered—so we began some chapters ago. The people of the mountains, often to their grave dislike, have found themselves the objects of surveys and studies, the subjects of pictures and articles in newspapers and national magazines, the grist for the TV cameraman's mill as he grinds out pictures of poverty, malnutrition, ignorance, and loss of hope. The governments of the mountain states have suddenly awakened to the needs of great numbers of their people who have been lost to their consciousness for so long. The Federal government has its programs, and there is every reason to believe that these will grow ever larger in scope and cost as the nation increasingly comes to see this great segment of its people in trouble. The mass migration of more than 2,000,000 people from Appalachia to our cities has awakened school, welfare, housing, and law enforcement officials to the problems of Appalachian people in their midst and in their native homes. Pilot programs by government and by private foundations are multiplying. A person working in the area becomes more and more confused with which one to involve himself. If nothing else, he wishes not to stand in the way of change.

THE FORCES OF CHANGE

The forces of change are under way and, no doubt, will pick up speed as the next few years pass. The folk culture is under tremendous pressure to change—yes, even to pass out of existence, for those who work in Appalachia, not understanding the values of the culture, will try to destroy the folk customs and the culture and force the Southern highlander into the conforming mode of the rest 'of America. There is something about a dominant culture which will not allow a differing culture to exist side by side with it. So long as the Southern mountaineer lived apart in his labyrinth, he was left alone. As he begins to emerge from the mountains, or as middle class America begins to invade his homeland, these well-meaning citizens feel that the mountaineer, on seeing their "superior" culture, will immediately want to share it. For many a mountaineer, nothing could be farther from the truth, as I shall try to point out later in this chapter.

Whether the mountaineer wishes to change or not, forces have been unleashed that tend to make him change. His geographic isolation, long a barrier to his finding a place alongside his counterpart in other parts of the nation, is being destroyed as new roads begin to reach their fingers into the labyrinth to draw him out. Many a mountaineer who, a generation ago, was hopelessly cut off much of the year even from the nearest town, now finds himself nearer and nearer to all-weather hard-surface roads. These roads take him out year round and bring others in with goods and services, information, and culture that are samples of a life he never knew. Television brings him face to face with modern American culture (a most unfortunate way to express this), and both he and his children spend hours watching and unknowingly absorbing the ideas and values piped into his very front room. More and more every mountain shack or coal-camp house sprouts its TV antenna on chimney or pole.

The pressure of economics has forced the children to leave

home for the cities. While this migration is full of heart-
aches and broken spirits and often frayed nerves and nervous
breakdowns, it has nevertheless provided some open doors,
some incentive, some hope of a better life for the young. So
long as migration is a possibility for the mountain person,
giving him an opportunity, at least, for achievement, the
forces of change for his culture are powerful, for as his ties
with home are strong, the migrant returns often to the
mountains. Many a highway from city to mountains is
crowded on Friday and Sunday nights as the migrants
spend weekends at home and then return to their work.
These contacts of the city dweller with his mountain kin
are a great force toward change. A number of the young
people with whom we have worked during the years stop
in to visit us when they return at Easter or Memorial Day
or Homecoming. Time and again they say, "When we lived
here, things always looked so good to us. But now when we
come back we suddenly see how bad it really is."

For several reasons, the birth rate in the mountains has
been falling steadily. In the first place, the migration of the
young couples has left the area with an increasingly aging
population. Economic needs have forced parents to rethink
the problem of the size of their families. And the spreading
knowledge of birth-control methods, the reduction in their
cost, and the simplicity of their use have all reduced the
size of the Southern mountain family. Because there are
fewer children, the family circle is harder to maintain and
scarcely provides enough persons to compose a reference
group of satisfactory size.

The new emphasis on education is also reaching slowly
into the mountains. More and more young people are fin-
ishing high school and going on to college. While the rate
is still much below the national average, each advancement
is a significant force for change. The presence of a bach-

elor's degree and an occasional doctor's degree in the mountaineer's family tends to make him think differently toward
the educated man. Even though I doubt that the educational level of rural mountain areas is increasing much, since
most of the better educated youths continue to leave, still
the impact is felt. In our own area, an illiterate father now
has a daughter with a master's degree from a state university. That is a great jump in one generation. I would
not say this is at all common; yet it is happening—and education opens doors in people's lives.

The fact that the child of the mountain family no longer
is an economic asset also forces a change. The mountain
child was formerly expected to grow up quickly in order to
help in the hard life of the family. That necessity is almost
past. He now has leisure. His fewer home tasks free him
—or could free him—for school and community activities
that mold him in directions other than those of his close-
knit home. He is also free now to visit his relatives in cities
during the summer.

The changing role of male and female is having a profound effect on the folk culture. As the mountain man has
been more and more eliminated from the job market, his
strength being no longer needed, the mountain woman has
found her place in hospitals as a practical nurse or assistant,
in assembly plants where her nimble fingers and ability to
stay at routine jobs over long stretches of time stand her in
good stead, as store clerk where her more social nature has
given her an advantage over her less social husband. Although this situation has been a tremendous blow to the
mountain man, who once ruled his house as a king, it has
been a great boost to the mountain woman, as new opportunities and experiences open before her. This change in
the role of the sexes has forced a great change on the structure of the folk culture of the Southern mountains, and will

continue to do so. The very fact that the mountain woman is using her energies outside the home strikes at the heart of the reference-group structure. The freedom and independence she gains from having her own money to spend and her own life to run, instead of being at the mercy of her husband for both, will bring a new force to bear on the mountain family.

If the programs of the Federal and state governments in Appalachia are even fairly successful in bringing in new industries and tourists and in encouraging retraining of workers, such developments, too, will open doors of opportunity which will alter the folk culture of the mountaineer. If the mountain culture has developed its particular nature because of closed doors, then opening the doors should alter it by weakening its foundations. This will not happen overnight, or even in a generation—as it has with foreign immigrants. With the immigrants the first generation clings fairly closely to the pattern of life of the old country, even though the circumstances that molded their culture are not operating here. But in the second generation the great change is evident, as the forces of the new society in a new land begin to take hold in young lives. The second-generation mountaineer, however, cannot experience this free break with the old culture of his parents, since he may still live enmeshed in the traditional patterns that have molded his ancestors.

OBSTACLES TO CHANGE

Lest we think that all the forces in Appalachia are moving in the direction of change, it is necessary to mention that there are also powerful counterforces that resist change and even strengthen the folk culture itself. These forces are at work not only in the Southern mountains, the homeland of the mountaineer, but also in the inner city to which he moves with his family. This inner city, too, tends to be a kind of "closed door" society. Opportunities for employment are limited, for the mountain man's few skills and little education enable him to get only the low-paying and insecure jobs. The inner city, too, becomes a kind of labyrinth where he gets lost in the maze of people and buildings and traffic. Here he can be cut off again from the opportunity of steady work, adequate income, health services, good education, and an environment which can be stimulating. The inner-city family shares a good many of the mountaineer's cultural characteristics. This, then, is an obstacle to change. The mountaineer often simply changes places of residence when he moves to the city. The forces that mold him are much the same in either place.

The second obstacle to change is within the mountaineer himself. He does not want to change. He has found his way of life satisfying enough, and he looks on persons of other classes without a trace of envy or jealousy. He does not want to be like them. It is important for us who work with those in the folk or working class to know and understand this. We too easily assume that everybody wants to be upwardly mobile. Those who seem disinterested just need to be motivated or enabled to do so, we think. Yet, the folk- or working-class person is satisfied with his way and style of life. All he lacks—or thinks he lacks—is enough money to live reasonably well.

The third obstacle is the resistance of the reference-group structure to change. It has its own built-in pressures to conform and punishments for those who defect. Combine the difficulty of getting a new idea into the reference group with its expressed hostility to what it takes to be the goals of middle class culture, and you have a tough combination to beat. The mountaineer rejects the status-seeking, social-climbing, "get rich," let's-have-fun orientation, which he pictures as middle class, while at the same time fearing to associate with people he feels are "above" him.

The fourth obstacle to change is found in the nature of the security pattern of the folk culture, in which one's identity and purposes are intimately bound up with particular persons. The mountain man does not "advance" or "better himself" by moving out of the reference-group culture; he just cuts himself off from the people who give his life its meaning. As Marion Pearsall puts it, "Practically everything valued in traditional family routine is at variance with the only available alternative, the largely impersonal and arbitrary regulated culture of the machine age with its emphasis on technological proficiency. Little wonder that ventures into that other world do not effectively break the bond with the family-based world."[1]

The fifth obstacle to change is quite recent, yet growing. The great release valve for the Southern mountains has been the possibility of migration. One-fourth of the population has left the region in the past two decades—two million people. Without this release, the situation today would be much worse than it is. Most of these migrants have been able to find relatively satisfactory employment and a reasonable life in the cities inside as well as outside the region. Within the past four years the situation has begun to change. Before this time there was the possibility, at least, of mountain families' finding work in the cities, but more and more this door, too, is closing to them. The cry of the nation's industries for high school graduates only has eliminated great numbers of mountain men and women; nobody wants them. Even the mountain youths who have finished high school are really not much wanted, for their education is not so good as that ob-

[1] *Little Smoky Ridge* (Tuscaloosa: University of Alabama Press, 1959), p. 169.

tained outside the region, nor do mountain schools have many technical courses available. The job market is already overfull, and mountain youths are no longer needed for the factories and mills of an economy that is automating at an accelerating pace. In the spring of 1964, our church, in co-operation with the county school board, took a group of high school boys to a large city on a "go-see" trip. Several of the very large companies refused to show the boys through their factories, on the grounds that they did not want to encourage young people to come to that city. Already they were laying off hundreds because of automation—they wanted no more youths to compound the problem.

This is a formidable obstacle indeed. When the possibility of migration closes to the mountaineer—when automation forces many who are at or near the bottom of the job ladder to return to their mountain homes—the folk culture will be resumed, more in earnest than ever. The mountaineer who bore the brunt of the industrial revolution first on the farm and then in the coal mines will be hit again, as the factories to which he fled repeat the process of automation at his expense. Once more the door of opportunity will close for him and for his inner-city counterpart, pushing them back ever harder toward the reference group, toward fear, other-worldliness, and the other characteristics portrayed in this study. Only a miracle or a revolutionary change in our social and economic ideology (which would also be a miracle) will prevent this from happening.

SOME BEGINNING POINTS

Whatever our diagnosis of the mountaineer's problem might be, those of us who believe in action must move ahead. We cannot wait passively while history works itself out. I could well call the following discussion "clues for action," since in my own field—religion—no group has really been successful in the mountains; what we have done is to acquire a number of clues, beginning points, and suggestions for effective work. I believe that these observations, which are made largely for persons from outside who are coming into the area, are equally valid for workers who are native to the area.

[1]   Our programs must be developed with two groups in mind—those who are upwardly mobile and may wish to move out of the area and the culture and those who choose to remain within it.

Work with the upwardly mobile is, naturally enough, what middle class persons and organizations concentrate on and do most effectively. We find young persons who have object-oriented goals, and we do all we can to see that these goals are reached. These are the "success" stories that fill reports to home offices, mission boards, and the like, in the hope that they justify the expenditure of resources. It is of course true that when outside leaders provide the kind of challenge and support that enables young people to achieve object goals, they have performed an important task—and have done something personally satisfying as well. But, unfortunately, a few families resettled, a few scholarships awarded, a handful of small businesses given a start is not a creative and constructive program for Appalachia.

The really hard part of the task is trying to reach the people who do not have what seem to us worthwhile goals, who do not give any sign of wanting to improve their lot in life and resist all attempts at change. These persons have great personal needs that must be met before very many social needs can be tackled. Fear, a tremendous sense of inadequacy, difficulty in expressing oneself, inability to handle personal differences, almost antisocial behavior in groups other than one's own—all these prevent group paticipation.

In approaching these problems, we are the ones who must adapt. We must be able to understand the people better than they understand themselves and, in order to draw them forth, be able to enter into their ways of acting and looking at things. Up the hollows, to this row of houses, to that small settlement, to this lone family we must reach out, suffer rebuff, and reach out again. We have to be willing to go to them even when they are not willing to come to us. In *Little Smoky Ridge*, Marion Pearsall gives an example— a typhoid-immunization clinic that ended up as a mobile, house-to-house affair, since very few of the citizens would come to a central spot.[2]

This approach takes almost impossible amounts of time —just talking on the back porch or by the roadside, waiting in silence with a family during times of bereavement, stopping to visit when you happen to be by the house: personal interest, personal involvement, personal help. It takes a long time to become adept at this person-oriented work. Outsiders tend to be in too great a hurry to get things done, programs organized, statistics compiled.

I put this clue first because I believe it is the most important one. Whenever the mountaineer senses that we are not really interested in him as a person—whenever we begin treating him in object-oriented ways—he feels that he is being used, and right there the progress of the work stops. He may not rebel openly; more than likely, he will simply be silent and uncooperative, and we will not know why. Persons on our own staff have had to learn that this time spent "hand-holding," as we have called it, is not wasted— that we really are accomplishing something when we are just interacting as persons.

[2] We must be prepared to work within the present structure of life and culture in the mountains. We all tend

2 Pearsall, pp. 157-60.

to assume that our particular style of life is better than that of others, but we must not keep wishing all the time that the people were more like us. I must admit that I don't want anybody setting out to change me—and neither does the mountaineer. In a great many ways he is perfectly happy with his culture; it expresses his goals and desires quite adequately. Because he is happy with it, he wants other persons to like it, too. A question often asked of a visitor is, "Well, how do you like it here?" or "What do you think of us hillbillies?" The people desperately want to be liked for the way they are—and we cannot work with them unless we *do* like them. Horace Kephart put it this way: "Those who would help them must do so in a perfectly frank and kindly way, showing always a genuine interest in them, but never a trace of patronizing condescension."[3]

Ministers must remember that the Christian faith is not a culture, and must not try to impose particular church organization and life patterns on mountain people any more than Western Christians should seek to impose Western culture on Orientals when they become Christians. In any field we must be ready to analyze the entire range of our activities, distinguishing between those things that have no class connotations, those that have class connotations which are necessary to function and fulfillment, and those that have class connotations which are merely refinements and are not necessary to function and fulfillment. As an example, the kind of language we employ is important. The mountain man uses terse, simple Anglo-Saxon words, not long Latin words. His vocabulary is astonishingly limited, and he has trouble understanding involved sentences and nuances of wording. Likewise, we must not expect to have much success if we try to conduct meetings according to

[3] *Our Southern Highlanders* (New York: Outing Publishing Co., 1913), p. 209.

Roberts' *Rules of Order*. Mountain meetings must be informal, with few sharp votes taken and plenty of time allowed for the sense of the group to come out. In a meeting a mountaineer will not stand up and openly disagree with an educated leader. Usually, he will simply be silent —his standard defense in stressful situations. Or he may say, "You do whatever you want to." And when the time for carrying out the plan arrives, he simply doesn't show up. In any event, long-range planning does not interest him. We, the outsiders, must have the long-range plans and move the mountaineer along one decision at a time. Certainly we have to think in terms of "five years from now," lest the slowness of the pace utterly discourage us.

A good example of working within the mountain climate comes from the Planned Parenthood organization sponsored by our church. One of the community representatives, "a woman to whom other women talk," has done a first-rate job of spreading information about birth-control methods. She talks with women, gives them thorough explanations, and is faithful in keeping supplies for them, but she simply cannot fill out the reports and forms that are required for each family. Maybe she can't write well, maybe the forms confuse her, or maybe she just can't see the need for them. Whatever the reason, this failing must be accepted in her, and someone on the central committee must get the information from her and make out the reports, while patiently attempting to train her—which may or may not be possible.

[3] We must promote varied forms of intergroup cooperation—between communities, clubs, agencies, churches. Paradoxically—in view of the Church's teaching—in many communities the deepest divisions among the people are along church lines. Those who go here have no dealings— in any field—with those who go there. Of course, so long

as the mountaineer operates chiefly on his feelings, he must be led slowly and gently into any kind of new association. A desire for an overall strategy must rule as many churches as possible, so that churches of several denominations can be yoked under one minister—a *trained* minister—interdenominational parishes are formed, interchurch cooperation is fostered. Such a development would affect all facets of the mountaineer's life; it could gradually provide the wider social outlet that he needs.

[4]   The church must be ready and willing to provide a ministry to the whole man. Let me illustrate this point by relating an incident that occurred at one of the local family reunions. It was a hot day, and many relatives had come distances to be there. One man who now lived in a city buttonholed me under a tree to tell me how much our particular church had meant to him and his family during the years they had lived here. The church had supplied clothing when they were hard pressed, it had provided food when they were hungry, it had provided for medicine and care when they were sick.

"Yes, sir," he said, "Whenever I needed help I always came to your church." Then he added, "But when I wanted religion, I went to my own."

While we could not (and would not) provide the kind of action-centered, emotionally labile church service that he felt necessary, we were able to offer the help he could find nowhere else, and this is a legitimate ministry. There are few other agencies in these outlying places to which the mountaineer can turn—which is one reason I stress here the significance of the church. In many a mountain community the trained pastor is the best educated person and the only one with both knowledge and concern who can act as liaison between the people and potentially helpful groups outside. The church must be willing to accept this use of his time and abilities to add to the total leadership resources of the community. His role must not be limited to the carrying-out of church-centered activities. Whatever can be done to provide necessary health services, planned-parenthood information, recreation, education, counseling, or community development leadership is a vitally valid outgrowth of the Sunday church service.

[5] Incoming organizations must help local persons grow and develop. Because mountain people lack the skills for social encounter and interaction, there is a great temptation for the trained person simply to do what needs doing rather than to train someone else. This attitude of "doing for" people must be fought vigorously. As it is, the mountaineer tends to be a pessimistic person, faced as he has always been with ample reasons to be so. He tends to give up too easily, with a "What's the use?" attitude. Persons who are able, and there are many, must be prodded to take responsibilities, but then must be given the skills and encouragement which enable them to carry on. There will be need for a great deal of encouragement along the way and, of course, recognition for achievement.

Through our churches we have relocated a number of families in various cities, families who had been emotionally unable to move on their own. It took hours of counseling and encouraging these families to make the move, but most of them did so satisfactorily. Sometimes it meant that the receiving city church had to help them know how to shop in a supermarket, where to get medical, dental, or other kinds of help, how to get children enrolled in school, or even how to use the city bus system and other simple things that city people take for granted. Only occasionally were the relocated families "our church" families, but this is the kind of ministry to the whole community that all churches must undertake.

Most of the young people must one day migrate to the cities if they are to find work. They must prepare themselves for the kind of work there is to do; yet an unusually high percentage of the boys have never even been outside the mountains, nor will they finish high school. They simply do not know what to expect in the city. Hence we have taken bus loads of ninth- and tenth-grade boys to industrial cities to live for a few days with city families, to hear civic and industrial leaders speak, to visit the plants and to meet mountain people who are now living in the city. These were not "our church" boys, but were chosen by their teachers as being likely to benefit from such an opportunity. Since the school did not provide it, we felt we ought to let them "go-see" in order to enable them to prepare better for what lies ahead.

[6] Outsiders must provide stimulus. The mountaineer's life is amazingly tradition bound. The reference group, as we know, resists all inroads of change or new ideas. The school system and the political setup (and what else is there in many mountainous areas besides these two institutions?) are both home grown and traditional. Incoming groups can provide much-needed stimulation, as can the church, if it is not bound by the culture.

We cannot advocate radical changes, lest we alienate ourselves from the very people we hope to serve. But if the culture of Appalachia has been formed by one door closing after another, who is to begin opening doors? Who is abler than community-action groups and churches to provide new opportunities for people both in learning how and in doing? Mountaineers have by circumstances been trained to be people without tongues. The provision of ways to express themselves gives them confidence in their own abilities and worth. They learn how to be a part of society by actually taking part. This may be in community action, as the church takes the initiative in beginning a Scout troop, in repairing playground equipment, or in building a sidewalk to the school. It may be in local community development. It may be on a larger scale, area development or regional libraries or bookmobiles. It may be in organizing groups to demand better health or welfare or police services in their counties. I once heard that it may be possible to learn to swim without ever getting in the water, but it is not very likely to happen.

There will be some controversy, of course. Anyone who wants to avoid it had better stay out of Appalachia altogether. Many times indigenous leaders can do far more than those from the outside, since they already understand the culture from the inside. These leaders may be persons who are upwardly mobile, or who have already moved out of the culture yet who have great feeling for it, having an empathy for both the old and the new culture. They will probably have much more rapport with the people than middle class professionals. Such persons are not easy to find, however. Often the upwardly mobile who have moved out of the culture reject it completely. It may be necessary for the "outsiders" to develop the programs and have skilled and trained "insiders" carry them out. These persons may well become the mediators between the classes and perform services which are unique in that they reach best those who need them most.

[7] The last clue comes in the form of an admonition: "Don't expect things to happen in a day!" There are many good things about the mountain culture which are not immediately apparent to the newly arriving, impatient worker. We must not jump in to make changes too hastily, for we may well destroy that which is good. An ever increasing number of outside influences are tending to break down the isolation and backwardness of the area. The great dino-

saurs disappeared from the earth not one by one, or through great and intensive effort. They disappeared because the climate changed. Let us make sure that the climate changes in a direction we choose. While things are moving slowly, let us begin to guide the mountain man toward wholeness. If he does not find meaning for his life, all the gains that may be his will be nothing.

EVALUATIONS AND CONCLUSIONS

An objective evaluation of the mountain folk culture or any other subculture—including one's own—is extremely difficult to make, since we are all prejudiced in favor of our own cultural tradition. The very fact that we are a part of a particular subculture strongly suggests that we either are happy enough to stay within it or else are not sufficiently attracted to other styles of life to be drawn to them. Another reason the various subcultures are difficult to evaluate is that each one expresses in the most basic ways the special values which that particular group holds and desires. Thus, evaluation of a subculture would require making a value judgment of the goals, hopes, and aspirations of that group of people—a matter that few people could ever agree on.

For example, the professional class family organization allows each member of the family to develop his own particular interests, talents, and aspirations. If one member of the family wishes to excel in playing the violin, another wishes to travel extensively, and still another wishes to become involved in community activities, each is encouraged and helped to accomplish his aim. To mountain people this would be no family at all, but simply a collection of separate individuals. Their goals have more to do with interrelatedness as persons, which would, to the professional class family, be purposeless and defeating to personal achievement. Thus, one's own philosophy of life, purposes, and hopes must be evaluated if a subculture is to be evaluated.

It is possible, however, to note some general strengths and weaknesses of the mountain folk culture as it faces the kind of a world the twentieth century presents. I would hope these limited evaluations might not reflect too strongly my bias toward the particular subculture of which I am a part. Nor, as I mention what I feel to be the serious deficiencies of the mountain culture, am I going to claim that my own style of life has no problems. There are, indeed, many advantages to the folk culture which modern-day America might well wish to share.

Part of the mountain population can be described as lower class. This segment of society tends to exhibit many of the same characteristics everywhere. As was pointed out in Chapter 1, it is a pathological society in that it does not deal adequately with the problems of life. It is not a problem-solving society—in fact, it is a problem-creating society. It does not foster the human values of personal worth, dignity, responsibility, and happiness. The persons within it have failed to make life adjustments of the most basic kinds, and these failures are perpetuated. Family life is such that attitudes and habits are fostered which almost guarantee defeat for its members, and these family habits are passed on from one generation to the next. This class creates the most problems—mental illness, alcoholism, drug addiction, and instability of character. Because the lower classes receive far less adequate care than other groups, persons sink ever deeper.[4] This class produces people who can work only in unskilled jobs and are therefore increas-

---

[4] August B. Hollingshead and Frederick C. Redlich, *Social Class and Mental Illness: A Community Study* (New York: John Wiley & Sons, Inc., 1958), chapters 9 and 10.

ingly unwanted by the American economy. The spiral goes down and down, each problem reinforcing the others. Many of these families are multiple-problem families, having a number of serious situations to face, any one of which would be difficult for even a well-adjusted, adequate-income family to handle.

Examples of such families in the Southern Appalachians flood to my mind. One such family has six children. The parents have little education, having been brought up in homes far up the hollow. Neither has had any contact with life outside the valley. The poverty and insecurity of their childhood caused both the husband and the wife to have severe health problems. The husband, for example, has very poor eyesight—not poor enough to qualify him for welfare, yet too poor to enable him to pass a physical for a job. They married very young, and the children came close together. There was no prenatal care for the wife, and only emergency treatment was possible for the children. One child has rheumatic fever, one had a nervous breakdown while still in elementary school, another has poor eyesight like his father, another has such severe bleeding ulcers that at the age of twenty-one he is unemployable. None of the children has finished school.

Appalachia has a growing number of such families, who are further from solving their problems now than they were a generation ago. Our system of welfare reinforces their plight, rather than creatively trying to provide positive solutions. At the very moment that I was writing this paragraph, a woman from one of the hollows rang our doorbell. Her story was simply a repetition of one I have heard a thousand times. Her husband was laid off in the mines. His educational level is sixth grade. They have eight children, one a small baby. They exist (if that is the word) on $165 a month, received from work on a government road program. "Why do they keep having children when they can't afford them?" we ask. Because they do not know anything about planned-parenthood methods—that is a luxury for the better educated and higher income people. "Why do they waste their money on pop and other nonessentials?" we ask. Because life lived in a family of ten on such an income is almost unbearable, and after a time these families just give up trying. The odds against them are too great. Let any family of ten anywhere in the United States try to live on $40 a week, and see what kind of life results. See how despair, poor health, alcoholism, mental illness, and instability multiply. See how soon a family just gives up when there is absolutely no hope of anything better.

I would hesitate to say how much of Appalachia falls into this category—the lower class. Probably much more than we would care to imagine. People stranded in rotting coal camps or in tiny houses off the main roads and up the hollows—old people living on $35-a-month welfare checks, or couples living on less than twice that much. There they live without hope, abandoned by a nation that doesn't really know how to spend all its wealth, and so lavishes vitamins, health foods, and fancy clothes on its animal pets. There they live, with not a soul to help, with no one to call to in their trouble, repeating generation after generation the failures of their fathers.

It is this lower class, not only in the mountains but everywhere, which will require our greatest effort if we are to give them real, meaningful help. It contains those who are most fearful, most suspicious of outsiders, most difficult to reach. And these are the people who probably would want to move out of their class into another if they could be enabled so to do. Yet they are also the people who do not have the skills, resources, and education that would enable them to move out, and their present income guarantees that they will never be able to—unless they are given the necessary economic and human resources.

There are no advantages to this lower class—only disadvantages. Massive amounts of professional skill, understanding, and financial help will be required to admit it to the folk culture in the mountains or the working class in the cities—the first step in its progress. The middle class, with its object-orientation, is still a long way off. This we must understand, we who work with lower class people. Escalation to middle class is scarcely even a remote goal for these people.

The part of mountain culture that is folk class, that has met the situation of mountain life in an adequate fashion, although in ways different from those of middle class culture, has its inadequacies too, as I have shown elsewhere. I do not, however, characterize this subculture as wrong. It developed to meet particular needs, but it is now seriously inadequate to prepare its people for the cooperative, interrelated, technical society into which we have moved in the twentieth century. One of its most serious defects, and one from which others stem, is the extreme resistance to new ideas—which effectively squelches not only the ideas but those who bring them. In centuries past, when change came slowly over the generations, the traditional-minded person was not far removed from the great thoughts of his leaders. In our day, when changes of revolutionary scope occur within a generation, the tradition-bound person finds himself hardly living in the same world with his forward-looking counterparts in the rest of society. Ways and means must be found to help the mountaineer open his life toward the future.

The mountain culture is inadequate in its very permissive child-rearing practices, which produce lives based almost totally on personal feelings. Life in a complex society simply cannot be lived successfully with this kind of orientation. Young people should not be brought up to feel, for example, that they can quit school because they don't like a particular teacher—as happens now. A great deal of work must be done with parents to help them set goals for their children toward which home training can enable them to move—goals which the children and youth take for their own and toward which they strive.

Lack of goals is destructive of human initiative and creativity. Its effects are reinforced by the pressure of the reference group against all who would rise above the group. Mountain society fails to build into its people a desire for excellence in anything, except sports! Only those who are upwardly mobile, who do not depend so thoroughly on acceptance by the reference group, set goals and work toward them. The others conform, fit in, give in. A young boy who showed some interest in studying the formation of the mountains and the various strata began a rock collection. His mother said, "I finally shamed him out of it. Imagine a boy doing that!" There is great need, in short, to help mountain youth set and keep object goals to strive for.

Young people who accept even limited goals are then more open to learning the social skills necessary to participation in society at large. They are increasingly freed from the restrictions of a security found only in family and reference group. Many boys and girls are afraid to be away from home even overnight, and their parents encourage this clinging. They can hardly be said to be preparing for life in a mobile society. It is all very well to have an attachment to place and family, but this debilitating dependence the mountaineer can no longer afford. Even if young people cannot leave the region, because of automation in the cities, they will need new attitudes in order to receive the kind of life that will continue to encroach upon the hills. Thus mountain youth need experiences and contacts outside the area. The "ingrown-ness" of education, religion, and other youth-molding forces must be increasingly broken down.

Encouraging the upwardly mobile person is surely one of the significant contributions that social agencies can make. Schools, churches, and all manner of community and fraternal groups must work unceasingly at helping those who wish to move out of the culture become strong persons who can live apart from the group and achieve in their own right. This task requires personal encouragement, interest, and friendship. It may also require providing scholarships, job openings, or even living arrangements outside the area. It is not easy to step out of the security of reference-group society, where no demands are made on one, and those who do try need much strengthening in the attempt.

The reference-group culture is seriously inadequate in preparing children for the kind of schooling needed in a technical society. The mountain child learns early to grasp the nuances in personal relationships, which is a good and desirable thing in an increasingly impersonal society. This is one of the charms of mountain people. But the child must also learn to grasp ideas, concepts, abstractions, which are all conveyed by words. As it is now, he learns only to hear the feeling of the words. Therefore planned learning experiences must be offered to young children to prepare them for school. Unfortunately, few counties have kindergartens or nursery schools. It is ironical that the middle and upper class neighborhoods of the nation, where the children least need such facilities, are most likely to have them. One first-grade teacher told me that she even has to teach some of her pupils what books are before they can be introduced to reading. They have never had the joy of owning a single book or of having one read to them. In a world of books, is it any wonder the mountain child is behind his city counterpart?

Reference-group society has the disadvantage of splitting the family into groups divided by age and sex, thereby severely limiting its teaching influence. For example, parents have little influence in the youth reference groups; they exercise only a sort of negative control. Youth standards are set by other youth, and the group is closed to direct adult influence. This is a serious handicap to the young people, who are at an age when they could benefit greatly from adult stimulation and challenge. Community and church organizations need to seek to "invade" these youth reference groups, providing creative spare-time recreations and stimulating adult contacts. Organizations must also set up activities in which the whole family may participate in some kind of meaningful way that will bind them together with more than merely emotional ties. Too many mountain families do nothing creative together, and those who wish to are thwarted because they do not know what to do.

Another of the serious faults of the culture is the inability of its people to work together, or even to see the need for doing so. The mountaineer must be helped both to see the need for cooperative work and to develop the skills necessary for it. Ways must be found to engage him in larger groups than his own small area has afforded in the past.

Since the culture inadequately prepares its members to relate to "outsiders," there is a great need for "bridge" persons, who can help the suspicious and fearful to respond more positively to the persons and institutions which will increasingly be of help and resource—doctors, psychiatrists, clinics, hospitals; goverment in the form of agency officials, policemen, public health nurses, welfare workers; and such caretaker persons as clergymen, social workers, and recreation leaders. The mountaineer's suspicion of these persons limits his use of them to crisis occasions, when, in fact, their purpose is to be of assistance in many ways at other times. He needs help in understanding that government and other institutions cannot be run in person-oriented ways but must be conducted in great measure on an impersonal objective basis. He needs help in seeing that a certain amount of bureaucratic organization is a necessary thing, and that a government does not exist for an individual person's benefit. A good many of us in every culture need such training, too, of course.

Some of the ways in which the social structure of the mountains is inadequate in the world of today have been enumerated. I have dwelt upon them in order to help the above-mentioned outsiders—who will be discovering Appalachia for themselves—to understand the culture more quickly and to build upon its real advantages.

There are aspects of mountain life which might well be adopted by persons now living the over-organized, distressfully busy lives characteristic of our overall society. Let the outsider consider seriously before he rushes in with preconceived notions of how to get the mountaineer to improve (translate: "be like us"). Mountain people have a deep feeling of belonging and of loyalty. They are unashamedly glad to be mountaineers. They are at home here in a unique way. They belong to a family, a valley, a county, a state. They know they belong, and others know it, too. The rootlessness of a society on the move is not found here.

In its less extreme aspects, the person-orientation of the people is refreshing in an America that becomes more and more willing to assign one a number. Here you do know your neighbors (almost too well!), and they know you. Store clerks know who you are and treat you as a human being; service station employees give extra service to please you. There is time to talk and make friends. A former resident back from New Jersey for a visit put it this way: "Up there, they are different from us. Here I care for you and you care for me. We know each other and help each other. There it's 'hooray for me, and heck with you.' "

People in the mountains are not driven by the clock or the appointment book. "The only people who run here are you preachers," someone once said to me. My wife and I knew that we had accepted the society when we bought a porch swing and found the time to sit in it on a long summer evening, enjoying the quiet and beauty of the mountains around us.

There is an independence from the pressures of the world —no "keeping up with the Joneses,"—no social climbing. The avid and grasping materialism which is apparent in some places is absent here. A man is satisfied with what he has at the moment. Granted, this lack of striving has been carried to an extreme, but a certain easing of the pace is welcome.

The old are not shuffled off in a corner to die alone. If the immediate family cannot care for an aged person, sometimes friends in the community will do it. Many times an old person lives in his own little two-room house as long as he is able, with family and friends to "look about him" several times a day. Care of the bedfast may not be as efficient as that in a nursing home, but it is far easier on the old, who are most accustomed to folk ways. Even though the care of an elderly invalid often works real hardship on the family, nursing homes are seldom resorted to. Such care is considered part of one's duty to parents—almost a payment for care received in one's infancy.

Perhaps the greatest advantage of the folk culture will become evident in the cybernetic age to come. Much of Appalachia has slept through a revolution, having missed the whole industrial age with its competition, with its idea that the meaning of life is found in work, that education is only to prepare one for one's work, that money is the measure of success. This has been a restless age, in which men have driven themselves by the clock and the calendar, retiring in their sixties to rot quickly away because they have never learned how to live unless they are working. Only the coal-producing areas of the southern mountains were affected by the industrial age, and even these sections caught scarcely more than a glimpse of it. Their exposure did not last long enough for them to be caught up by its spirit and molded by its pressures.

Thus the mountaineer has not had drilled into him the virtue of working for the sake of work. He can sit on his front-porch swing and be content, not having to be up doing something or creating something. He can spend time with a clear conscience. I do not want in any sense to romanticize the mountaineer's situation, but I do want to suggest, as others have done, that perhaps the mountaineer will be more ready to enter the cybernetic age (in one leap from the agrarian age) than those who are deeply enmeshed in the industrial age. When that time comes fully upon us, when machines take the toil out of work, when long hours are not required of industrial workers, when making a living does not require life's main strength, the mountaineer may well be ready to move into the situation more easily than the rest of us. The cybernetic age is coming rapidly—the age when we must redefine the worth of man in terms other than the nature of his work and the size of his income. Making such a redefinition will not be easy, for it will require a complete change in our concepts and our philosophy of life, as well as in our activities. When our life situation becomes transformed by the cybernetic revolution, it may well be that the mountaineer will already have the concept of life and work fit for the new age.

Appendix

Middle Class American	*Southern Appalachian*
PERSONAL CHARACTERISTICS	
1. Emphasis on community, church, clubs, etc.	1. Individualism; self-centered concerns
2. Thoughts of change and progress; expectation of change, usually for the better	2. Attitudes strongly traditionalistic
3. Freedom to determine one's life and goals	3. Fatalism
4. Routine-seeker	4. Action-seeker
5. Self-assurance	5. Sense of anxiety
6. No particular stress on maleness	6. Stress on traditional masculinity
7. Use of ideas, ideals, and abstractions	7. Use of anecdotes
8. Acceptance of object goals	8. Rejection of object goals
9. Oriented to progress	9. Oriented to existence
10. Strong emphasis on saving and budgeting	10. No saving or budgeting
11. Desire and ability to plan ahead carefully	11. No interest in long-range careful planning
12. Placement of group goals above personal aims	12. Precedence of personal feelings and whims over group goals

13. Recognition of expert opinion

13. Expert opinion not recognized

Family Life Characteristics

14. Child-centered family

14. Adult-centered family

15. Responsibility for family decisions shared by husband and wife

15. Male-dominated family

16. "Togetherness" of husband and wife

16. Separateness of husband and wife; separate reference groups

17. Home tasks shared by husband and wife

17. Sharp delineation of home tasks between husband and wife

18. Many family activities shared (vacations, amusements, etc.)

18. Few shared family activities

19. Disciplined child-rearing; stress on what is thought best for the child's development

19. Permissive child-rearing; stress on what pleases the child

20. Family bound by common interests as well as emotional ties

20. Family bound by emotional ties; few common interests

21. Family a bridge to outside world

21. Separation of family and outside world

Relationships With Others

22. Reference group less important

22. Reference group most important

23. Object-oriented life pattern

23. Person-oriented life pattern

24. Association between sexes

24. Little or no association between sexes

25. Strong pressure of status

25. No status seeking

26. Striving for excellence

26. Leveling tendency in society

27. Readiness to join groups

28. Ability to function in objective ways in a group

29. Attachment to work; concern for job security and satisfaction

30. Emphasis on education

31. Cooperation with doctors, hospitals, and "outsiders"

32. Use of government and law to achieve goals

33. Acceptance of the world

34. Participation in organized amusements, cultural activities, etc.

27. Rejection of joining groups

28. Ability to function in a group only on a personal basis

29. Detachment from work; little concern for job security or satisfaction

30. Ambivalence toward education

31. Fear of doctors, hospitals, those in authority, the well-educated

32. Antagonism toward government and law

33. Suspicion and fear of outside world

34. Rejection of organized amusements, cultural activities, etc.

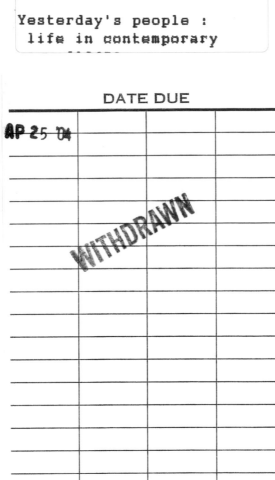